Arctic Ocean

ASIA

DERSEN
RDE
• BISKUPIN

OPE   Aral Sea

VESUVIUS
• POMPEII   • TROY
               • PRIENE

Mycenae   • EBLA   Khorsabad   Lo-yang •   HEIJOKYO   ASUKA
CORINTH   • Nineveh   CHANG' AN •   NARA   • FUJIWARAKYO
      Sidon • Tyre   NIMRUD
   Jerusalem   Assur
   Jericho   HATRA
         • PETRA
      • EL-AMARNA
Deir el-Medina • Thebes   • MOHENJO-DARO
                                       • ZAWAR

• Lake Chad
                          VIJAYANAGARA •   ANGKOR •   Pacific Ocean

RICA

                          Indian Ocean

                                                                          AUSTRALASIA

REAT ZIMBABWE •

ANTARCTICA

ABANDONED PLACES

ABANDONED
PLACES

LESLEY ADKINS
AND ROY ADKINS

CHARTWELL
BOOKS, INC.

A QUINTET BOOK

Published by Chartwell Books
A Division of Book Sales, Inc.
110 Enterprise Avenue
Secaucus, New Jersey 07094

ISBN 1-55521-679-X

This book was designed and produced by
Quintet Publishing Limited
6 Blundell Street
London N7 9BH

Creative Director: Peter Bridgewater
Art Director: Ian Hunt
Designer: James Lawrence
Project Editor: Caroline Beattie
Editor: Susan Baker
Picture Researchers: Lesley & Roy Adkins

Typeset in Great Britain by
Central Southern Typesetters, Eastbourne
Manufactured in Hong Kong by
Regent Publishing Services Limited
Printed in Hong Kong by
Leefung-Asco Printers Limited

This book is
dedicated to
Vera Parker and
Ivy Robinson

Contents

Lost and Found

"THE RUIN"

Wrǣtlic is þes wealstān; wyrde gebrǣcon
burgstede burston; þrosnað enta geweorc,
Hrōfas sind gehrorene, hrēorge torras,
hrīmgeat berofen hrīm on līme
scearde scūrbeorge scorene, gedrorene,
ǣldo undereotone. Eorðgrāp hafað
waldendwyrhtan, forweorone, geleorene,
heard gripe hrūsan, ðþ hund cnēa
werþēoda gewitan.

"Well-wrought this wall: Wierds* broke it.
The stronghold burst...
Snapped rooftrees, towers fallen,
the work of the Giants, the stonesmiths,
mouldereth.

      Rime scoureth gatetowers
        rime on mortar
Shattered the showershields, roofs ruined,
age under-ate them.

        And the wielders and wrights?
Earthgrip holds them – gone, long gone,
fast in gravesgrasp while fifty fathers
and sons have passed..."

           (Trans. Michael Alexander)
*the Fates

LEFT *A marble relief sculpture depicting a fox and grapes from the Roman city of Corinth, which replaced the previous city destroyed in 146 BC.*

Such are the words by which an anonymous Anglo-Saxon poet began describing the abandoned site of a Roman city in the 7th century AD. From clues in other parts of the poem, the city has been identified as that of Bath in England, which became deserted in the 5th century AD and was captured by the Saxons in AD 577. Throughout history, abandoned places have held a fascination for many people. This has often found expression in art: ruined buildings in deserted landscapes are a common subject in paintings, and abandoned places are treated in a variety of ways in prose and in poetry.

Travellers coming across ruined buildings in jungles or deserts naturally wondered how they came to be there, and why they were deserted and ruined. The writings of explorers and travellers contain accounts of many deserted places in distant lands, while the work of archaeologists has shown that the remains of many abandoned places can in fact lie close at hand, literally under one's feet.

The discovery of abandoned places over the centuries has occurred in a number of ways. Apart from sites which have become completely buried or sufficiently ruined as to be unrecognizable, few have been lost completely. Some buried sites may have been anticipated as a potential archaeological site before they were identified with a known historical place, as in the case of Troy, which is described later in this chapter. In many cases, then, the "discovery" of an abandoned place is a rediscovery, or a recognition of the true nature of the site. Stonehenge, for example, was abandoned for many centuries, its true history long forgotten, and myths and legends evolved to explain the origin of such a curious ruin. Only in the 18th century did scholars begin to speculate seriously about who built Stonehenge and for what purpose. A temple, built either by the Druids or by the Romans, was the accepted and often-

....
BELOW *The trilithons consist of two stone uprights and a lintel across the top, held in place by mortise-and-tenon joints carved in stone. They date to around 2000 BC and are only found at the site of Stonehenge in England. The site was for many centuries a bleak, remote abandoned place on the sheep downs of Salisbury Plain, only frequented by shepherds and the occasional artist and traveller. It is now a major tourist attraction.*
....

debated theory, which was not to be significantly revised until the second half of the 20th century. We now know that Stonehenge went through several phases of construction and alteration, was in use for well over a thousand years, and began to be built around 3100 BC, some three thousand years earlier than had been thought by those who had attributed the site to the Druids. Stonehenge, though, is still regarded as a temple (although nowadays the term "ritual site" is used), and we have very little further knowledge of what took place at Stonehenge than did the 18th century antiquarians. The ruins are now world-famous, attracting hundreds of thousands of visitors each year, and it is difficult to imagine a time when the site was abandoned and deserted.

In some places, whole areas became deserted, so that sites were completely lost, to be truly discovered at a later date. One such place was Petra. This ancient city in the Arabian desert was only known to the local desert tribes, who regarded the ruins as "works of infidels", and whose only interest in them stemmed from a hope of hidden treasure. Consequently, it was left to Jean Louis Burckhardt, who was exploring the area disguised as an Arab for safety, to discover and report on the lost city.

Other places, particularly those that have been destroyed by war or natural disasters, became so ruined or buried as to be unrecognizable, and their remains have only been discovered through archaeological excavation. The Bronze Age city of Akrotiri, on the Greek island of Santorini, was

ABOVE *The 2nd century* AD *Roman theatre at Petra in Jordan, behind which are tombs cut into the soft pink sandstone. This remarkable site was a true "lost city", only re-discovered in 1812 by Jean Louis Burckhardt. The theatre consists of 33 rows of seats cut from the rock, with stage buildings in the foreground.*

ABOVE Excavated buildings of the Bronze Age city at Akrotiri, on the island of Santorini, Greece. The city was abandoned and buried after an earthquake and a huge volcanic eruption in the mid 2nd millenium BC. It was discovered by chance in the late 19th century.

FAR RIGHT The temple of Apollo at Pompeii in Italy is situated by the forum and consists of a colonnade of 48 columns. A copy of a bronze statue of Apollo the Archer has been set up on the site where the original statue was found. The original statue is now in Naples Museum.

RIGHT A plaster cast of a dog from Pompeii in Italy. It died struggling with its chain, by which it had been tethered, in the House of Vesonius Primus.

completely buried under ash and rock during a volcanic eruption in the middle of the 2nd millenium BC. Chance finds of the remains of buildings in the late 19th century led to an archaeological excavation which established that they belonged to a past civilization which lay buried there. It was not until the much larger-scale excavations of the 1960s and 1970s, though, that the importance of the ancient city was appreciated, with sensational finds of buildings and artefacts, preserved by their burial under the debris from the volcano. Unlike Pompeii, bodies were not found in the ruins, showing that the city had been abandoned before it was engulfed.

Pompeii, near Naples in Italy, was another city buried during a volcanic eruption, and there are many superficial similarities between Pompeii and Akrotiri. The location of the Roman city of Pompeii, though, was

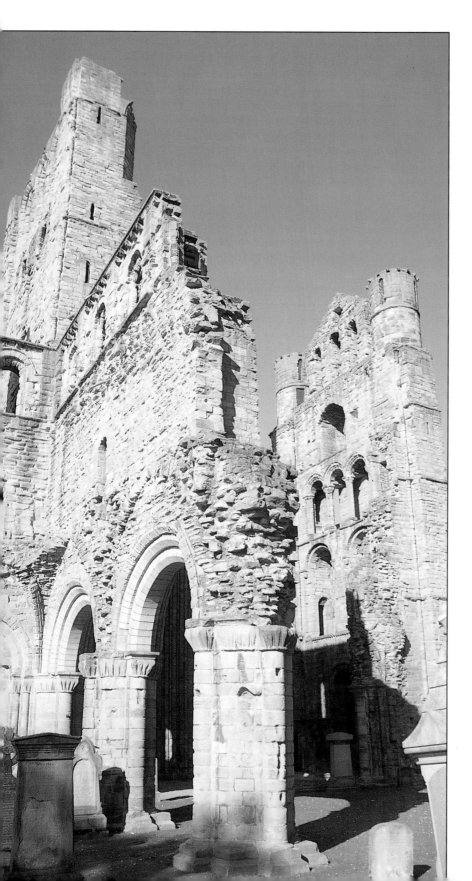

not totally forgotten, because references to the city and its destruction survived in the works of classical authors. A graphic account of the destruction of Pòmpeii in AD 79 is given in a letter written by Pliny the Younger to the historian Tacitus, where he describes the rain of cinders, "then pumice-stones, and stones scorched, blackened, and cracked by fire" which fell on the area. It is clear from his account that many of the inhabitants were overcome by poisonous fumes before they could escape, with the result that excavators of the site, many centuries later, were able to make plaster casts of the hollows left in the ash by the bodies of the victims.

In many places, the destruction or disuse of a site led to its abandonment for a period of time, before the area was used again at a later date. Often this later occupation involved much clearance and new construction work, but usually some reuse and rebuilding of the ruins as well. Wherever this process has occurred, the resulting remains form a confused pattern that is difficult to sort out by excavation alone. For example, the Roman city of Londinium went into decline and was probably abandoned around the end of the 5th century AD. It does not seem to have been occupied again until the beginnings of the Saxon and Medieval town of London some centuries later. In the intervening period, the archaeological evidence suggests only small rural settlements in the area and casual occupation of the city, perhaps by passing travellers, but there are no documentary sources to shed light on the problem.

In contrast, the history of Corinth on the Greek mainland is known from the writings of ancient authors. Although the remains of ancient Corinth that are visible today are a mixture of classical Greek and early Roman architecture from the city that Julius Caesar restored as a Roman colony in 46 BC, it is known that the original Greek city of Corinth had been devastated by the Romans a hundred years earlier in 146 BC.

Some places, although abandoned, have never been lost completely. This is particularly true of places abandoned in relatively recent times, when at the very

LEFT *A monastery on the island of Lindisfarne, England, was abandoned in the 8th century because of Danish raids. The ruins mainly belong to a later monastery.*

ABOVE *The ghost town of Bodie in California, USA, has long been uninhabited, but the site was never lost. It is now a State Historic Park, and its surviving buildings are just as they were when they were abandoned.*

least there are documents, and often maps, showing the location and layout of such places. The gold rush town of Bodie in California, for example, grew up specifically to serve the gold miners, but once the gold rush was over, it was abandoned, never to be re-occupied. The site was not lost, however, and today the place is a State Historic Park, preserved as an example of a ghost town left over from the 1849 Gold Rush.

The discovery of many deserted sites in remote places has often happened by chance. A good example of this is the discovery of the ruined cliff dwellings at Mesa Verde,

Colorado, by members of the Wetherill family. The Wetherills were a Quaker family from Pennsylvania who set up a ranch in Colorado in 1880. On 18th December 1888, Richard Wetherill and his brother-in-law Charlie Mason were searching for stray cattle in Cliff Canyon, and having climbed up to a vantage point for a better view, spotted the ruins of Mesa Verde in a massive cave in the opposite wall of the canyon. The family were already interested in the Indian remains that they had seen in the area, but it was this chance discovery that led Richard Wetherill in particular to explore the whole area, discovering similar sites. This eventually led him to pursue a career of excavation, discovery and artefact collection.

Often lost sites have been discovered, not quite by chance, but at least unintentionally. Explorers have set off in search of one place of which they have heard, only to discover another unknown place. Machu Picchu, for example, was discovered by Hiram Bingham in his search for Vilcabamba, the last capital and fabled lost city of the Incas. In his search for Vilcabamba, Bingham explored various Inca sites in the Peruvian Andes. The Incas were very powerful from about AD 1200 until the arrival of the Spanish in the early 16th century when the Inca civilization was destroyed and many settlements were abandoned.

Machu Picchu, the so-called "lost city of the Incas", lies on a ridge between two mountains at a height of around 2750m (9000ft). On both sides of the city the land falls away in a series of man-made terraces

LEFT *The cliff-dwellings at Mesa Verde, USA, were discovered by chance in 1888. The main settlement consisted of over 200 rooms and 23 kivas built against the cliff face. The site was occupied from about AD 600, but was deserted towards the end of the 12th century.*

ABOVE *The remarkable Inca ruins at Machu Picchu, Peru, incorporate much evidence for architectural methods. The technique of close-fitting stonework is thought to have been first used in the construction of terraces for agriculture on Inca sites.*

before becoming a sheer drop to the valley nearly 600m (2000ft) below, where the river Urubamba flows around three sides of the site. It is a walled, fortified city, with a single entranceway approached by steep stone steps from the road to Cuzco. When he found the site in 1911, Bingham named it Machu Picchu after the mountain which overshadowed it. Initially Bingham thought that the city was a refuge of the Inca Chosen Women, or Virgins of the Sun, and this was supported by the preponderance of female skeletons buried in caves, but he later concluded that it could be identified as the first Inca settlement, Tampu Toccu, and also as Vilcabamba, the last refuge

....
RIGHT *A view through the serpent's window in the Temple of the Sun at Machu Picchu, Peru. Fine Inca architectural construction can be seen, with stone blocks fitted together precisely without the use of mortar.*
....
BELOW *Machu Picchu in Peru is one of the world's most spectacular abandoned sites. It is located on a ridge at a height of some 2750 m (9023 ft), and was discovered in 1911.*
....

of the Incas following the Spanish conquest. It was later shown by Gene Savoy that Machu Picchu was neither Tampu Toccu nor Vilcabamba, and that the real ruins of Vilcabamba lay at Espiritu Pampa (ironically a site which Bingham had rejected as a possible site of Vilcabamba). Nevertheless, Bingham had managed to discover and explore several Inca sites abandoned since the Spanish conquest, not least of which is Machu Picchu itself. Machu Picchu remains an enigma. The site belongs to the late Inca period, but was abandoned well before the arrival of the Spanish in 1532, and was never found by them. It may not be the "lost city of the

ABOVE *The mound at Hissarlik in Turkey was identified by*
Schliemann as that of the legendary Troy. He proceeded to
excavate this complex site which has evidence of many phases
of occupation spanning hundreds of years.

Incas", but it is certainly one of the world's most evocative abandoned places.

In some cases, the search for specific places which have been abandoned and lost, but whose previous existence was known, has been dramatically successful. Probably the most striking instance of this is the discovery of the site of Troy in 1870 by Heinrich Schliemann. A German self-made millionaire, Schliemann was fascinated by the *Iliad* and the *Odyssey*, and was convinced that these poems of Homer depicted real people, real events, and real places, whereas previously

....
BELOW *One of the buildings belonging to the many superimposed settlements at Troy, in Turkey, which Schliemann was unable to unravel sufficiently with his methods of excavation.*
....

the poems had been regarded as, at best, a vague and stylistically exaggerated view of ancient Greek history. By using clues in the Homeric poems to identify geographical features, Schliemann came to the conclusion that a mound at Hissarlik in Turkey was the site of Troy. Excavation proved him correct, and he went on to excavate other Homeric sites on the mainland of Greece, at Mycenae, Tiryns and Orchomenos.

With much of the world's land surface at least superficially explored, there are likely to be few visible sites left for the explorer or

traveller to discover for the first time. However, many more buried abandoned sites are discovered each year, either by accident, when construction work, quarrying or agriculture reveals the remains of a previously unknown site, or more frequently, by *archaeological survey*. In simple terms, archaeological survey is the deliberate search for unknown sites, and by far the most powerful tool for archaeological survey is air

BELOW *Nowadays construction work such as road building is more likely to reveal evidence of buried ancient sites than the accidental discovery of places still visible above ground.*

photography. From the air, sites can be seen which cannot be recognized from ground level, and photographs of newly-discovered sites from the air not only demonstrate their existence, but also help archaeologists to pinpoint them accurately.

Many once-abandoned places, particularly those with spectacular ruins, have become tourist attractions, visited by thousands of people each year. The pastime of visiting

ancient abandoned sites has largely developed since the 18th century, when a tour of Europe to look at art, antiquities and classical sites was considered desirable to complete a gentleman's education. This fashion led to a wider appreciation of archaeological sites – which then began to appear in the arts. Abandoned places, particularly if they had picturesque ruins, became the subject of many paintings and drawings. The sites were often given a very romantic treatment, especially in those paintings done in the early 19th century, with ruins set in an empty landscape, under a dramatic sky, with perhaps a shepherd and a flock of sheep, a band of travellers, or another artist sketching the ruins to give a human dimension. Wherever artists travelled, they found suitable landscapes to paint, and in the late 18th and early 19th centuries, abandoned places with romantic ruins were the height of fashion. Many such paintings and drawings are of classical sites in Greece, but the same treatment was given to places throughout Europe, and as far afield as Easter Island in the Pacific.

RIGHT *Visiting ancient abandoned places has for long been a pastime. The re-enactment of ancient activities such as archery is fast gaining popularity as a way of bringing a site to life and understanding how the site functioned in its heyday.*

ABOVE *In vast countries like the USSR, detailed survey and aerial photography is likely to reveal hundreds of previously unknown sites. This ancient Sogdian city in the Pamir mountains in Tajikistan was plundered and burned by Arabian invaders in the 8th century* AD.

The romantic view of ruins also gave rise to the use of deliberately constructed ruins in landscape gardens, and in the 18th century in particular, many landscape gardens in Britain were furnished with mock Roman arches, ruined castle towers and fragments of mock Gothic buildings. These ruins were generally screened by woodland so that people walking in the garden came upon them unexpectedly – mock abandoned places, set for repeated "discovery" in the microcosm of the landscape garden.

Deserted ruins have served to inspire poets, and throughout history poets have speculated about abandoned places; what they were like when they were flourishing, and what caused them to be abandoned. Poets have also frequently been influenced by the often melancholy and sometimes romantic atmosphere that such places can evoke. A poet may have been writing soon after a place had been deserted, such as the Chinese poet Ts'ao Chih. Writing at some time around the 2nd century AD, he laments the destruction of the war-ruined city of Lo-yang:–

"...A thousand miles without the smoke of a chimney.
I think of the house I lived in all those years:
I am heart-tied and cannot speak."

Other poets approach the subject from different directions. Mary Webb, for example, in her poem *Viriconium*, describes the wheat field where all that is left of the Roman city of Wroxeter is "one rent and mournful wall" which "yet towers

....
ABOVE *Particularly in the 18th century, landscape gardens were often provided with imitation ancient buildings, some deliberately constructed in a ruinous state. This Gothic temple was part of the early 18th century gardens at Painshill, England, designed for Charles Hamilton.*
....
LEFT *The large Roman town at Wroxeter in England now lies deserted beneath open fields. One single wall unaccountably survived, and is usually referred to as "the Old Work". In the 19th century much of the public baths was exposed, and modern excavation of the site is continuing.*
....

unscathed". A E Housman also muses on the site of Roman Wroxeter in his poem *On Wenlock Edge*, but he takes a more personal view, comparing himself and his feelings with the old inhabitants of the city.

Another poetic approach is to use the abandoned place as a springboard for the imagination. In his poem *The Deserted Village*, for instance, Goldsmith peoples the place with a milkmaid, schoolmaster, old soldier and various other characters, and contrasts their previous life in the "sweet smiling village" with the deserted site where "desolation saddens all".

Poetry, more than any other art form, expresses the widest possible range of responses to abandoned places. At one end of the spectrum is the expression of mourning at the recent destruction of a place such as in the 10th century Persian poem about the ruined city of Tus, near the Turkestan border:–

"Last night by ruined Tus I chanced to go
An owl sat perched where once the cock did crow
Quoth I, 'what message from this waste bring'st thou?'
Quoth he, 'The message is woe, woe, all's woe."

At the other end of the spectrum is the poet apparently inspired by only a fleeting glimpse of a place, as in Charles Johnston's Air Travel in Arabia:–

"Then Petra flashed by in a wink.
It looked like Eaton Square, but pink"

....
BELOW *A*bandoned sites *may not always be visible, but may be buried below ground level. Their excavated remains may be at least as informative as those sites with spectacular surviving monuments, even if they are not so picturesque.*
....
RIGHT This *triumphal arch, often called the Arch of Germanicus, leads into the forum of the ancient city of Pompeii, Italy.*
....

Abandoned places also occur in prose literature of various kinds. Apart from the obvious writings of explorers and travellers, and the accounts of fieldwork and excavation by archaeologists, deserted sites often appear in novels and short stories. Some works have used abandoned places as settings against which some of the action takes place, such as in Lord Lytton's *The Last Days of Pompeii*, or in *The Naulahka*, where Kipling uses the deserted Indian city of Chitor. In other stories, a site is chosen as a setting to heighten the tension at a crucial point, such as in Thomas Hardy's *Tess*

of the d'Urbervilles, where Tess, having killed Alec d'Urberville, is finally captured at Stonehenge, just as the sun is rising.

Most works of fiction, however, usually employ an imaginary site, and gothic horror stories, ghost stories, adventure stories, and thrillers have all made use of imaginary abandoned places. In some cases, though, it is clear that the imaginary site is based, however loosely, on a real place. In *King Solomon's Mines*, for example, Rider Haggard drew inspiration from the ruins of Great Zimbabwe, while sixteen years earlier, in 1869, HM Walmsley published *The ruined cities of Zululand* which gave a fictional account of a journey to these ruins.

The 19th century was the heyday of abandoned places in literature and art, but they still occur in the popular media of today. Films as diverse as the *Indiana Jones* and *James Bond* films on the one hand, and the film version of EM Forster's *A Passage to India* on the other, have all made use of abandoned places and deserted ruins as settings for part of the action. Consequently, some people have become accustomed to the idea of abandoned places in remote and exotic areas waiting for discovery and exploration, when in reality most such places have at least been discovered, if not thoroughly investigated. What we should consider is the fact that many more abandoned places, some perhaps with impressive ruins, still await discovery – not in far-off foreign countries, but down the road, across the way, or even in our own backyard, buried in ground that we pass by every day.

Power of the Elements

Although natural disasters can sometimes occur suddenly, causing sites to be abandoned very rapidly, environmental disasters are usually slow and insidious, and cause a site to decline gradually, but eventually leading to its abandonment. In many instances it is clear that such changes in the environment have actually been caused by people, through factors such as over-exploitation of agricultural land and deforestation.

MOHENJO-DARO, PAKISTAN

Quite often it is very difficult to determine, from the archaeological evidence alone, why a site was abandoned, but archaeologists are increasingly looking to environmental factors rather than accepting more simplistic explanations. The Indus Civilization collapsed around 2000 BC, and many sites, including Mohenjo-Daro, fell into disuse. It is now thought that man's over-exploitation of the region may have been the main cause.

The ruined city of Mohenjo-Daro ("Mound of the Dead") was once a major urban centre of the Harappa Culture or Indus Civilization, an Early Bronze Age civilization which flourished in the north-west of the Indian sub-continent in the second half of the 3rd millenium BC. Mohenjo-Daro is situated on the right bank of the Indus river, about 400km (250 miles) north of Karachi. It was discovered in 1922 by R D Banerji of the Archaeological Survey of India, and large-scale excavations took place for several years from 1924. About one-tenth of the city has been excavated.

The early origins of the site are unknown. Because the water table has risen, the early deposits are now waterlogged and have not been excavated. The main walled city of Mohenjo-Daro appears to have been laid out

RIGHT A steatite Indus seal depicting a bull found at Mohenjo-Daro. The short inscription may record the name of the merchant, and is an example of early writing.

LEFT The settlements in Chaco Canyon, USA, once supported a thriving agricultural community from about AD 950 to 1300. Recent falls of rock at Pueblo Bonito have damaged some of the ruins.

on a grid plan in about 2500 BC and was a
major centre of trade and manufacture. The
city covered an area of at least 100 hectares
(half a square mile), and was built on two
huge artificial mounds – a higher mound
known as the citadel or acropolis, and a
lower mound. The lower mound was largely
residential, and hundreds of dwelling houses,
larger buildings and unpaved streets have
been found there. Many houses had more
than one storey, and most were constructed
of baked brick, of a standard size found
throughout the Indus valley at this time.

The citadel overlooked the lower mound
and had a large granary, administrative,
ceremonial and religious buildings, but no
sign of a palace. There was also a Great Bath
in the northern part of the citadel which may
have been used for ritual bathing, and
covered an area of some 1700sq.m (2000sq.yd).
It displayed sophisticated building
techniques, and the centre-piece of the
complex was a pool, unparalleled in cities
until the Roman period.

The sophistication of planning in the city is
in fact best seen in the infrastructure relating
to the water supply and effluent disposal
systems. The Great Bath was not a storage
tank for water since fresh water was supplied
by a network of over 700 wells. These were
cylindrical shafts several metres deep lined
with standard-sized baked bricks. The wells
were in use at a time when cities in Egypt and
Mesopotamia still fetched water from nearby
rivers and stored it in cisterns.

Not only was the supply of water from
wells unique, but even more astonishing, this

LEFT *Mohenjo-Daro in the Indus Valley has a regular system of streets. The buildings were constructed of baked bricks and often had more than one storey.*

ABOVE *The city of Mohenjo-Daro in Pakistan was abandoned around 2000 BC, and was only re-occupied in the 2nd century AD when a Buddhist stupa and monastery were erected on the citadel. The remains of the stupa now dominate the city.*

RIGHT *A terracotta female figurine of a mother-goddess found at Mohenjo-Daro.*

29

was integrated with a drainage system. Waste water and sewage from houses were channelled into a complex system of drains running along the streets. The drains were brick-built, 50–60cm (20–24in) below the surface of the streets, and had removable covers to give access for cleaning. There were also cesspools and soakaway pits. Most houses, besides having a well, also had an indoor bathing platform; this was a low brick basin of about 2sq.m. (2sq.yd), from which water flowed into a soakaway pit or into a drain in the street through an outlet in the outside wall. Many houses also had a latrine, again connected to the drainage system.

Mohenjo-Daro was abandoned around 2000 BC, although the reasons for this are unclear. During excavations, several bodies were found in the streets, and it was originally thought that the city had been sacked by Aryan invaders. Nowadays it is thought that a number of factors may have been the cause of the abandonment; in particular, over-exploitation of the land, chronic flooding caused by deforestation, and soil erosion may well have led to a much more arid and inhospitable landscape. The site has remained abandoned, except perhaps for squatters, although in the 2nd century AD a Buddhist *stupa* and monastery were erected on the citadel. These in turn were abandoned and today their ruins dominate the site.

In recent years Mohenjo-Daro has deteriorated through salt deposits in the bricks causing them to disintegrate. To save the city, a programme of conservation began in 1973, sponsored by UNESCO.

PUEBLO BONITO, UNITED STATES OF AMERICA

As the bodies found in Mohenjo-Daro streets gave an initially false impression of that city's end, so too the evidence from the dwellings of the Anasazi in south-west America. The first settlement to be found by Richard Wetherill at Mesa Verde had everything so well preserved in the dry conditions that it looked as if the inhabitants had just fled. Likewise, the numerous human remains, including some dessicated bodies, seemed to show that a massacre had taken place. However, along with sites such as Pueblo Bonito, it now looks as if environmental factors were a more likely cause of abandonment.

Pueblo Bonito ("pretty village") is one of the most outstanding prehistoric sites in the United States. It lies in Chaco Canyon, in New Mexico. This canyon is 24km (15 miles) long and up to 1.6km (1 mile) wide, and lies in the centre of a vast arid desert of sand, rock and mesa, but it once supported a thriving agricultural community. The area was occupied by the Anasazi, a prehistoric stone age people with no knowledge of metals. The introduction of crops from Mexico gradually led the hunting and gathering communities to live in villages, in particular cliff dwellings and *pueblos*.

The Chaco Canyon settlements flourished between AD 950 and 1300, and there were numerous pueblos – agglomerations of rectangular living rooms built close together and often arranged in several storeys or

LEFT Wood was used in the construction of buildings at
Pueblo Bonito, USA, and survives well in the arid conditions.
It is therefore very important for the study of
dendrochronology in the region.

ABOVE The Pueblo
settlement at Pueblo
Bonito, USA, is situated
in the 24 km (15 mile)
long Chaco Canyon, now
in the centre of a vast
arid desert.

terraces. Pueblo Bonito was the largest, and consisted of a D-shaped arrangement of over 800 adjoining rooms around a central plaza. The outer walls were four to five storeys high, and the whole structure was like a huge stepped apartment. There were also 32 *kivas* – circular sunken rooms used as sacred places.

The pueblos were free-standing structures, unlike the cliff dwellings, such as at Mesa Verde. Construction at Pueblo Bonito was of stone, earth and wood, and some of the best stone masonry of this culture survives here. The population probably gradually increased at this time, and at its peak Pueblo Bonito may have sheltered 2,000 to 5,000 people, and the whole canyon 10,000 people. The early period up to AD 1150 is known as the Pueblo II period, and after that as the Pueblo III period. In the latter period, sites generally became more fortified, and at Pueblo Bonito several outside windows and entrances were sealed.

The people who lived there were highly skilled, and many examples of their pottery, weaving and other crafts have been found. Metal was not known, nor apparently, the use of the wheel. No writing is known, although some pictographs have been found. The water supply was controlled by a series of dams and channels, and over 400km (250 miles) of roads linked the communities in the canyon. Roads have also been found on the plateau leading north to the Mesa Verde area.

Because wood survives in arid conditions, the area is very important for the study of *dendrochronology* (a dating technique using the

ABOVE *Pictographs (paintings) have been found on some rock faces at Pueblo Bonito, USA.*

growth rings of trees). Pueblo Bonito is most famous for having provided the wooden beams enabling Professor A E Douglass (1867–1962) to complete the tree-ring sequence up to the present day; sites such as other pueblo villages can be dated by comparing wood with his tree-ring patterns. Furthermore, through the study of dendrochronology, climatic fluctuations could be recognized.

In about AD 1300 Pueblo Bonito was abandoned. Tree rings for AD 1276-99 point to a long drought. It is likely that crops failed, erosion of the soil took place, and agriculture could no longer sustain the increased population. This undoubtedly led to conflict between the communities and may also have led to disease. The people were certainly not driven out by attackers, and the area remained abandoned for about 100 years.

Pueblo Bonito was discovered in 1849 by an American soldier, James Simpson, and from 1895 the site was examined by Richard Wetherill, the discoverer of the contemporary cliff dwellings at Mesa Verde. Because the buildings were open to the weather, they were partly ruined, but some have since been restored. The site is now a National Monument, visited by thousands of people each year.

THE SAHARA

Although factors leading to abandonment of whole areas can often be attributed to people's over-exploitation of the environment, at other times widespread natural changes in the climate can be the cause. Evidence shows that the Sahara region was once not the arid zone that it is today.

From about 11,000 BC the Sahara region became less arid, with very large lakes being formed – Lake Chad reached an area of about one million sq.km (400,000sq. miles). From about 9000 BC there is evidence of widespread hunting and gathering communities in the region, and for over 5000 years the landscape consisted of lakes, marshes, woodland and grassland, with probably up to 300% more rainfall than today. Many sites have been discovered with artifacts such as bone and shell fish-hooks and harpoon heads, as well as quantities of fish bones, indicating that fishing was very important. There is also evidence of a more settled existence by about 6000 BC, based on arable farming and domesticated animals. These early settlers have left behind huge numbers of rock paintings, including portrayals of wild and domesticated animals, especially cattle, most of which are now alien to the region, and which became extinct over time. Particularly well-known are the immense quantities of rock art of the Tassili n'Ajjer region of Algeria, which is a huge sandstone plateau. From about 2500 BC, however, drier conditions began to take over and the land became dessicated – the result being that the Sahara was once again depopulated.

In the Roman period the climate is thought to have been as dry as it is now, and yet the Sahara supported a thriving agricultural community, including villas and cities, with the population overcoming the problems of the environment. In the Libyan Sahara there are hundreds of stone castles or fortified farms (known as *gsur*) and less substantial sites located along the wadi edges. These are of the Roman period and date from the 1st century AD. Some had presses for olives and vines, and it appears that a highly complex system of water control was developed in the Roman period, which took full advantage of the intermittent rainfall, and enabled agriculture to be maintained. This system gradually broke down due to the political insecurity in the late Roman period, and an increased population and over-exploitation of the land led to a collapse of the agricultural system. The desert encroached once again, and small farms, villas and cities were abandoned to the desert following the conquest by the Arabs in the 7th century AD.

SABRATHA, LIBYA

Sabratha was one of the many cities along the north African coast which expanded during the Roman period as the hinterland thrived, but it was eventually abandoned as the Sahara desert took over once more. Sabratha was originally founded by the Phoenicians, probably in the 5th century BC, although little of this early settlement has been excavated. In 46 BC it was annexed by Rome and was granted the status of a Roman colony in the 2nd century AD. The city became extremely prosperous during the Roman period, and a trading office of Sabrathans has been found at Ostia. Most of the city's wealth was based on olives, grain and fishing, and also on goods brought in by the trans-Saharan caravans. Sabratha was sacked in about AD 363 by the tribes of the Austuriani, but recovered once again, although on a lesser scale. Under Byzantine control new walls were constructed but these enclosed a much smaller area. The city was abandoned after seizure by the Arabs in AD 643, and the ruins became covered in sand. Extensive remains of Roman date survive, including temples, basilicas, and various bath buildings, all constructed of sandstone. Numerous mosaics have also been found. Large areas of Sabratha were systematically cleared by Italian archaeologists between 1925 and 1942, resulting in the removal of many of the later deposits and structures. A theatre of Antonine date on the sea shore has also been uncovered and restored. The architecture at Sabratha was never as lavish as at Leptis Magna, though, because the city never had an imperial benefactor. The downfall of Leptis Magna seemed an even greater disaster because of the splendour which that city once displayed.

LEPTIS MAGNA, LIBYA

The city of Leptis Magna lies in a desolate part of Libya, 140km (90 miles) east of Tripoli. It was founded by the Phoenicians, probably in the 7th century BC, as a trading post, but very few remains of the Phoenician settlement have been found so far. After the destruction of Carthage by the Romans, Leptis Magna began trading with Rome, and eventually became allied to Rome. From the 1st century AD it began to flourish, and the early Roman town was laid out on a grid pattern, with public buildings constructed of stone. These early buildings included a forum, market, temples, and a theatre. In AD 109–10 Leptis Magna acquired the status of a Roman colony, and shortly afterwards during the reign of the emperor Hadrian a large bath building was constructed, nowadays referred to as the Hadrianic Baths.

Leptis Magna was the birthplace of the emperor Septimius Severus (AD 193–211) who lavishly endowed the city with many fine buildings, including a new basilica and a forum, 300 x 180m (320 × 200yd) in area. Another structure of this date was a four-way triumphal arch. At this time the harbour was rebuilt on a monumental scale, and to prevent flooding in the city and the silting up of the harbour, a large dam was constructed

RIGHT *The Capitolium temple at Dougga, Tunisia, was constructed in* AD *166–7. The large porch has four Corinthian columns at the front and one on each side.*

upstream to divert the course of the Wadi Libda. Another notable building in Leptis Magna is known as the Hunting Baths. These were built on the outskirts of the city and are a virtually complete example of a vaulted bath-house, preserved under desert sand for hundreds of years. Inside were wall paintings with hunting scenes from which the baths take their name.

From the 3rd century the city began to decline, due to some extent to the over-

ABOVE *Many of the north African Roman sites survive well, often preserved under the encroaching sand. Dougga in Tunisia was a fairly modest town set in the hills over 100 km (62 miles) south-west of Tunis.*

exploitation of the hinterland and to tribal unrest. The lavish new harbour was hardly used as it rapidly silted up, and is now the most well-preserved example of a Roman harbour. In the 5th century the city came under attack from the Vandals. Sand began to encroach on the city, and by the time the Byzantines occupied the city under the emperor Justinian from AD 533, much of it was already buried under sand. At this stage churches were constructed, as well as new city walls enclosing a much smaller area. In AD 643 the Arab invasion brought an end to Leptis Magna. The city was never reoccupied after its abandonment, but instead was covered by wind-blown sand from the Sahara which assisted the preservation of the remains. The position of Leptis Magna was forgotten in Europe until the site was discovered by a Frenchman captured by pirates in the 17th century. After this, the site was visited and casually plundered for two hundred years before controlled excavations took place this century.

BISKUPIN, POLAND

The attempt to overcome and live in harmony with a difficult environment is also seen at Biskupin, but here again the battle for survival was lost. The site of Biskupin lies in flat countryside on a peninsula in Lake Biskupin, near Gniezno, in north-west Poland. It was once an island in the lake, and was inhabited mainly in the Early Iron Age, from about 700 to 400 BC, by Lusatian settlers. It was a fortified settlement of a type fairly common within the region at this time. What makes Biskupin exceptional is the remarkable state of preservation of timber structures due to them being waterlogged for over 2,000 years. This has enabled a plan and a partial sideview of the structures to be drawn up. In addition over 5 million artefacts have so far been recovered from the site.

The site was discovered in 1933 by a local schoolteacher just as it was on the verge of being completely destroyed. It was found in

lakeside meadows and at the very edge of the lake, because the water level of the lake was much lower than was normal. Excavation began on the site in 1934, which lasted right up to the outbreak of war, and aroused national interest. During the war many records and on-site reconstructions were destroyed, and eight members of the excavation team died. The Nazi military authorities covered up the excavations with sand and the woodwork began to dry out and perish. After this bleak period, work resumed on the site in 1946.

Biskupin covered about 2 hectares (5 acres) and was enclosed by a rampart made of sand, clay and stones with a timber box-frame. The exterior was covered in clay. This rampart was 3m (10ft) wide and up to 6m (20ft) high. On the south-west was a gateway 8m (8.5yd) long and 3m (10ft) wide, from which an oak causeway extended 120m (130yd) to the lakeside. The ramparts were further strengthened and protected by a series of timber breakwaters consisting of oak stakes rammed in at an angle. On the inside of the rampart wall, a timber street encircled the settlement of tightly-packed straight rows of timber houses – over 100 houses in all. Each house had a porch and a main room.

After about 40 years, this settlement was destroyed by fire, possibly in a Scythian attack, and a smaller settlement was built inside the ramparts, but of poorer materials. About 80 years later, in the later 5th century, this settlement was also destroyed and burned by Scythian invaders, and abandoned. At this time Europe was subject to climatic

change, and along with the deforestation of the area, the water level of the lake rose and low-lying areas were flooded. There was intermittent occupation on the site after this date, but on a very much reduced scale, until the place was finally abandoned. The island vanished under the waters of the lake, but the water levels reduced in the 4th century AD, and the site was refortified and occupied until the early Middle Ages when the inhabitants moved to the present Biskupin.

Biskupin is thought to have had a population of 700–1000 people. The settlement was obviously carefully planned, and was a considerable undertaking, requiring vast quantities of timber. The buildings do not show any evidence of a social hierarchy, and it may even have been an egalitarian society with no chief. From the finds, there is evidence for domesticated animals, for fishing and hunting, and a wooden plough and other artefacts provide evidence of arable farming. Various industries took place on the site itself, including bronze and bone working.

Biskupin was not an isolated site: many other fortified sites existed in the area at this time but only Biskupin has been so well preserved. Nowadays Biskupin is a popular archaeological attraction, and is often referred to as the "Polish Pompeii". There is a museum complex and on-site reconstructions of the buildings, which attract thousands of visitors each year.

The major problem and challenge facing archaeologists now is the conservation of the exposed wood.

LEFT *Biskupin in Poland was a fortified Iron Age island site, and its timber structures have survived so well that there was enough evidence to allow accurate reconstructions of the houses, streets and gateway to be built for display to visitors.*

FEDDERSEN WIERDE, GERMANY

The eventual abandonment of a site due to increased flooding is also seen at Feddersen Wierde, where the inhabitants had tried to cope with the conditions by building mounds. Here the flooding seems to have been due entirely to a general rise in the sea level throughout the area at that time. During the Roman Iron Age there began to be periodic flooding of the coastline of Holland and northern Germany. Rather than abandon these low-lying areas, the response was to construct settlements raised above the surrounding land on artificially-constructed mounds of varying sizes. The accumulation of domestic debris and animal manure also led to the growth of these mounds, which are commonly known in Holland as *Terpen*, and in Germany as *Wurten* or *Wierden*. Despite the constant inundation and salination of farmland, an agricultural economy was maintained around these settlements.

Feddersen Wierde, near Cuxhaven, is one of the most well preserved and thoroughly excavated sites of this type. It began as a small hamlet occupying the clay marshes of the Weser estuary in the 1st century BC. The settlement was subsequently laid out in a radial design around a central open space on an artificial mound, with up to about 50 huts. The huts were all constructed of wood; the lower parts of the wattle walls of the huts and fences have been preserved through waterlogging. The houses were mostly of the long-house tradition, divided by partitions. The long-house included a cattle byre at one end which had stalls with wattle partitions and a central drain, a working area in the centre, and a living room with a raised central hearth at the other end. Near most houses there was a raised granary. A substantial three-aisled building may have been a communal hall. Several huts were used as workshops for such crafts as leather, bone and wood working. Numerous Roman goods found on the site indicate that there was trade with the Roman world.

Early in the 5th century AD there was severe coastal flooding from the North Sea, making the land too wet and salty to support agriculture. Feddersen Wierde was abandoned, along with other similar settlements, and the area did not revive until the early Middle Ages.

RIGHT *The second city of Priene was built on higher ground overlooking the harbour, and the acropolis was constructed on the natural cliffs to the north for fortification.*

BELOW *The view from the acropolis at Priene would once have been across the harbour towards the open sea, but Priene has since become landlocked by the silting up of the river estuary. The view is now across the valley floor of the River Maeander.*

PRIENE, TURKEY

While constant flooding can cause a site to be abandoned fairly quickly, the silting up and landlocking of sites which were once on the coast is usually a slow process, resulting in the *gradual* decline of these sites. Priene was a site that declined in this way. It was probably a very early Ionian Greek colony founded in the 9th century BC. It was sited at the mouth of the River Maeander. This early city was not very successful, and suffered constant harassment especially from Lydia and Persia. In addition, the port became unusable with silting from the river, and the consequent rise in the water level made the city liable to flooding. It was then abandoned, and no trace of this early settlement has been found.

It probably lies hidden deep under the silt.

A completely new Hellenistic city was founded on higher ground nearby, in the mid-4th century BC. It was built during the reign of Alexander the Great, and the city prospered, due mainly to maritime trade and agriculture. It is the best preserved example of a planned Hellenistic city. Like all newly-founded Greek cities of this period, it had a rectangular grid plan of streets. Extensive excavations, carried on since the 19th century, have revealed much of its layout and evidence for the buildings. Many inscriptions have provided useful clues about everyday life in the city.

Priene overlooked the harbour and the river estuary, and was ringed by defensive walls with arched gates. In the centre of the street grid were municipal buildings such as a market place (*agora*) surrounded by porticoes, a council chamber (*bouleuterion*), and a town hall (*prytaneion*). The bouleuterion is very well preserved and probably dates from the 2nd century BC. It measures 21m x 20m (23yd × 22yd), with rows of seating on three sides, and originally had a wooden roof supported on pillars. Other buildings included shops, a D-shaped theatre with tiered seating and associated stage buildings, and numerous town-houses with pillared courtyards. The main temple was dedicated to Athena Polias and was a gift of Alexander the Great. In the south of the city was a *gymnasion* (an open court for recreation) and a *stadion* (racetrack) with seating for spectators. To the north of the city were steep cliffs on which a fortified acropolis was constructed.

With the foundation of numerous Greek cities in Aegean Anatolia, more intensive agriculture took place which probably led to severe soil erosion. Sediment gradually filled the estuary of the river Maeander, so that from the 1st century BC Priene became landlocked, and the surrounding land became marshy and uninhabitable. Cut off from lucrative maritime trade, with declining agriculture, and with competition from the city of Miletus, Priene fell into decline. The population diminished and the city was finally abandoned after the Seljuk invasion of the 13th century. The coastline continued to move westwards, so that today Priene overlooks the Maeander valley rather than the open sea.

OSTIA, ITALY

The silting up of harbours can be devastating as it can disrupt the whole basis of a community's existence and force a place to be abandoned like Priene. But Ostia, the port of ancient Rome at the mouth of the Tiber, withstood many of these setbacks until disease also took its toll and made the area uninhabitable for over four hundred years. At Ostia and in the surrounding region, the existence of malaria is well documented in historic times, but in earlier civilizations diseases such as malaria are almost impossible to detect.

Ostia was once situated right by the coast at the mouth of the River Tiber, but it is now 5km (3 miles) inland. The earliest settlement was a fort of the mid-4th century BC, which had walls of unmortared tufa blocks 1.7m (5.5ft) thick and 6m (20ft) high. This fort covered an area of just two hectares (5 acres), and was established to protect Rome from Greek raiders. Ostia then became a naval base, and subsequently developed into a commercial port, with goods being transported to Rome up the River Tiber. In particular, corn was imported into Rome via Ostia, so that Ostia grew in importance and eventually expanded to an area of 64 hectares (160 acres). In the early 1st century BC, new walls were constructed to protect the city.

Even though Ostia prospered, the harbour was unsatisfactory and prone to silting, and large ships had to unload offshore. Puteoli harbour in the Bay of Naples was preferred. To improve the situation, the emperor

RIGHT *A mosaic at Ostia, in Italy, depicting corn merchants selling their wares.*

Claudius in the 1st century AD had a new all-weather harbour constructed three miles north of Ostia, which was a huge undertaking. The harbour was not particularly successful and many ships sank, as the harbour was still too exposed to the open sea and weather, and so in the 2nd century Trajan ordered an hexagonal land-locked harbour to be built. This harbour, called Portus, was further inland and therefore much more sheltered. It was linked to the Tiber by canal. Portus developed as a commercial centre and eventually eclipsed Ostia. Claudius' harbour is now inland, due to the silting up of the delta. It lies practically beneath the airport, and excavations have uncovered ships which were wrecked and abandoned in this harbour.

In the meantime, though, Ostia continued to prosper as a port and a commercial centre, as the new harbour just a few miles to the north seemed to attract yet more trade to this part of the coast. Over 60 offices

representing commercial associations from across the ancient world have been found in the *Piazzale delle Corporazione*, grouped in a square, and each identified by a trademark and inscription in a mosaic floor. Huge warehouses for the storage of grain were built, and over 800 shops are known to have existed. The first houses were fairly spacious single storey ones similar to those seen in Pompeii, but as the population increased, tenement blocks were constructed, mostly of unfaced brick. These were four to five storeys high, and many had balconies. No areas have yet been identified as slum dwellings, although such areas are known in the City of Rome itself. At its height, Ostia probably had 80,000 inhabitants.

From the 3rd century AD Ostia declined as a port, since the harbour at Portus was favoured, but Ostia the town did not immediately decline. Instead it became a fashionable residential area, and large wealthy houses were built. In the 5th

BELOW *The interior of a food shop in the Roman town of Ostia, in Italy.*

century, though, the decline began. The harbour began to silt up, and malaria became prevalent, both in Ostia and in the surrounding farmland, as irrigation broke down and malarial swamps formed. The ancient port became isolated from the sea and Ostia was gradually deserted, neglected and looted. In 830 Gregory IV tried to revitalise the area by founding a fortified village nearby. By 1756 there were only 156 inhabitants, and half a century later only a few convicts were kept there.

This unhealthy area became totally

....
ABOVE *Many of the early houses at Ostia in Italy were similar to those found at Pompeii. This is the atrium or hall with a mosaic floor. A basin is set in the floor beneath the roof opening.*
....

desolate and the ruins disappeared from view, half buried and covered by vegetation. Only the *Capitolium* (the temple dedicated to Jupiter, Juno and Minerva) was still visible in the Middle Ages. The Tiber used to run past Ostia, but in 1558 it changed its course after a severe flood. It was not until the late 19th century that the malarial marshes were reclaimed, and then the spectacular ruins at Ostia began to be uncovered. Nowadays much of the site has been cleared, and what is left of the town gives a vivid picture of life in a Roman city.

chapter three

Social Strife

Rioting, rebellion, and above all, war, are probably the most common reasons for the destruction and abandonment of sites. Many ancient cities were destroyed during wars, and sometimes the destruction is well documented in ancient literature, as in the case of the Roman destruction of Carthage.

CARTHAGE, TUNISIA

The earliest evidence of Phoenician settlement at Carthage dates from the 8th century BC, although ancient literary sources claim that the foundation of the city took place some years earlier in 814 BC. Carthage was originally a trading colony of the city of Tyre; Tyre and Sidon, on the Lebanese coast, were at that time the principal Phoenician cities. In the following two-and-a-half centuries, Carthage prospered and expanded, founding trading colonies of its own. By 500 BC it had been cut off from the eastern Phoenician cities, which had been taken over by the Assyrians, and from this point the people are usually referred to as Carthaginians. The Carthaginians expanded their operations during the 4th century BC,

LEFT *The temples at Angkor contained immense quantities of relief sculpture. This example depicts a battle between the Khmer (on the right) and the neighbouring Cham (on the left).*

setting up trading centres along the southern and western coasts of the Mediterranean. The city of Carthage itself expanded, exploiting the fertile agricultural land of north-east Tunisia. It was the wealthiest city in the region, and the dominant power in the western Mediterranean. Two harbours were built in Carthage in the 3rd century BC – one for the merchant fleet and one for the navy.

The rising power of Rome and the expansion of its influence inevitably led to a clash with Carthage, and the struggle between these two powers, known as the Punic Wars, continued for over a century. It was a war of attrition that Rome finally won, and Rome took over many of Carthage's colony cities and outposts. Carthage itself fell to the Roman general Scipio in 146 BC, and literary evidence records that the final stages of the assault saw bitter house-to-house fighting, with both sides setting fire to sections of the city as part of their strategy. Resistance was eventually crushed, but fires raged in the city for some days. Scipio collected all gold, silver and sacred objects for Rome and let his troops plunder the rest. Those who had surrendered were sold into

slavery, and everything still standing was demolished. Finally, Scipio formally cursed the site and a plough was symbolically drawn across the remains and salt sown in the furrow to show it was to remain barren forever.

The site did lay barren for over a hundred years until, ironically, the Romans themselves re-established a city there in 29 BC. As the port from which African grain and olives were shipped to Italy, Carthage prospered, becoming the second largest city in the western part of the empire, after Rome itself. The city was wrecked by the Vandals in the 5th century AD, and was later taken under Byzantine control in AD 533. It prospered again, for a while, but was already in decline due to a reduction in Mediterranean trade in the 7th century AD, when it was destroyed by the Arabs in AD 698. After this, the ruins were steadily plundered for building stone for the construction of towns on the North African coast; some of the stone was even used in the construction of palaces and cathedrals in Europe. The result was that by the time archaeological excavations of the site began in the 19th century, very few standing ruins remained.

The site of Carthage is now in the northern suburbs of modern Tunis and under threat from modern development. Amongst the modern buildings are remains dating from all the previous cities on the site. Parts of the two man-made Carthaginian harbours can still be seen, and Roman structures include baths, a theatre, and an amphitheatre.

LEFT Excavations at Carthage, in Tunisia, have been carried out in recent years, in particular to prevent information being lost through destruction of evidence by modern development with the encroaching suburbs of Tunis.

ABOVE The amphitheatre is one of the best surviving Roman structures at Carthage, in Tunisia. It would have once been one of the main centres of entertainment for the inhabitants.

THREAVE CASTLE, SCOTLAND

Another well-documented abandoned site is that of Threave Castle in Scotland. Just as the destruction of Carthage was the culmination of the Roman campaign to destroy Phoenician power, so the capture of Threave was the end of King James II's campaign to destroy the power of the Black Douglas, but in this case the castle survived, only to be destroyed during a later campaign against the supporters of Charles I.

Threave Castle is now an imposing ruin situated on an island in the River Dee, 2.4km (1.5 miles) west of the town of Castle Douglas. Archibald the Grim, the 3rd Earl of Douglas, is thought to have ordered the castle to be built after becoming Lord of Galloway in 1369, and the castle continued in the control of the Douglas family. James II (1437-60) was determined to destroy the power of the Black Douglas, and in 1455 he systematically destroyed all their major strongholds until by the beginning of June only the island fortress of Threave was still holding out. Surviving records give details about the subsequent siege which was attended by the king in person. A huge siege gun and other ordnance were brought to the site, but the garrison surrendered before the castle was taken.

The whole of the Lordship of Galloway was annexed to the Crown, including Threave Castle, which then passed through various custodians. Henry VIII attempted to gain control of Threave, which did pass into English hands for a brief period, until 1545 when it was recaptured by the Scots after a

ABOVE *Threave Castle in Scotland is situated on an island in the River Dee, and is still an imposing ruin, despite its deliberate destruction in 1640.*

LEFT *Inside the ruins of the main five-storeyed tower-house at Threave Castle in Scotland. The wooden floors have decayed, leaving just the shell of the building.*

short siege. The Maxwell family were then allowed to remain keepers, but Threave lost its importance as a fortress on the Anglo-Scottish border after the accession of James VI of Scotland as James I of England. By 1638 Robert Maxwell, Earl of Nithsdale, held Threave, and he was a supporter of Charles I. This led to the final overthrow of the fortress in 1640, after the Covenanters laid siege to the castle for 13 weeks, until the garrison surrendered. The castle was then demolished so that it could never be inhabited again. However, it underwent minor works in the 19th century to make it suitable for prisoners from the Napoleonic Wars.

The early castle built by Archibald the Grim was a 5-storied tower-house with only one entrance, and walls nearly 3m (10ft) thick. The main room – the hall – was on the third floor. Excavations have revealed that the tower-house was surrounded by several less substantial buildings. In about 1450, before the siege of James II, a masonry wall 5.5m (18ft) high was built round the tower-house as an artillery fortification. It had slits for firing long bows and cross bows, and three circular towers for small guns. Two of these towers were badly damaged in the 1640 siege and have since collapsed.

HASANLU, IRAN

Particularly with the most ancient sites, it is quite usual for no documentary evidence to exist, and it is only the archaeological evidence that can demonstrate the destruction and abandonment of a site. At

Hasanlu, for instance, excavation has shown that its destruction and abandonment were caused by an attack on the city in about 800 BC.

The mound or *tell* of Hasanlu lies in the north-west of Iran to the south of Lake Urmia, and dominates the northern Solduz valley, one of the few passes from Mesopotamia to Iran. Long-term excavations have taken place at the site since 1957. The tell was long-lived, being first occupied from the 6th–3rd millenium BC. The site consists of a central mound 25m (80ft) high and 200m (218yd) in diameter surrounded by a lower mound 600m (650yd) in diameter. The early prehistoric occupation was sited on the central mound. The later, outer town grew up around the base of the mound. In about 1000 BC the central mound was fortified as a citadel, while much of the outer mound was used as a cemetery and for the homes of the inhabitants.

The buildings so far excavated in the citadel were constructed on top of the debris of the much earlier prehistoric remains and may have been the palaces of successive rulers of the city. The impressive city walls and the buildings were constructed of sun-dried mud bricks and some limestone which was brought from a distance of 30km (20 miles). Some of the buildings had upper storeys. No written documents have yet been found, so the detailed history of the site is unknown. It may have been allied with the Assyrians, and in about 800 BC it was destroyed in an enemy attack, probably by the Urartians. There is vivid evidence of the burning and final

destruction of the site before it was abandoned.

Amongst the debris, numerous bodies of the defenders and looters alike have been found, many killed by collapsing roofs; one man was clutching a unique solid gold bowl decorated with representations of mythical scenes in relief. Skeletons of four horses were found in one destroyed building, and nearby a man lay by a pile of bronze harness fittings. There were other rich finds in the burnt citadel as well as finds from graves, such as artefacts of gold, silver, electrum, glass, and carved ivory, as well as numerous bronze bowls and iron tools and weapons, giving an indication of the high standards of craftsmanship. These finds and the evidence of the attack have survived because the site was destroyed and abandoned, leaving the site to remain relatively undisturbed for nearly 3,000 years.

EBLA, SYRIA

The evidence for attack, destruction and abandonment is seldom as clear-cut as it is at Hasanlu. Successive settlements at Ebla, for example, were destroyed and rebuilt at least twice before it was finally destroyed and abandoned.

Tell Mardikh, the site of Ebla, is situated by the River Oronto, 38km (24 miles) south of Aleppo. The tell is of an unusually large size, and unlike many other tells, the site was totally free of recent occupation or cemeteries. Because of this, Rome University decided to carry out excavations there from

RIGHT *Tell Mardikh in north Syria is now known to be the site of ancient Ebla. Excavations have uncovered a remarkable royal archive, preserved in the debris of a royal palace.*

1964 onwards. The site was not known to be associated with any documented ancient settlement, but in 1969 it was for the first time recognized as ancient Ebla, and continuing excavations have revealed it to be an extremely important site. The tell consists of an almost circular central mound known as the "Acropolis" and a huge flat area termed the "Lower City".

The site was first occupied in the 4th millenium BC, but its period of greatest wealth and power was in the mid-3rd millenium BC. The period from 2400 BC to 2250 BC saw the first great urban centre at Ebla. Little is known of the appearance of this first city, but on the Acropolis (which was lower than it is now) was a palace, and the Lower City must have been densely packed with private houses of mud brick. There was probably a city wall of stone. At this period Ebla was a prosperous trading centre, exporting woollen cloth, wood, and furniture far afield. It had about 250,000 inhabitants and was administered by a large bureaucracy as witnessed in the remarkable find of the state archives. One large Royal Palace of this period (palace G of Ebla IIB) has been excavated, and in 1975 the state archives were discovered. These consisted of over 15,000 clay tablets inscribed in cuneiform script, some written in a previously unknown language, now termed Eblaite. The tablets were originally carefully stacked on wooden shelves, but these had collapsed during the destruction of the palace, and remained in this position until recovered in excavation. Research on the tablets is continuing, but

already a great deal of information has been gained about the political organization, economy and religion of Ebla over a 140-year period of its history.

The settlement at Ebla was devastated in about 2250 BC, probably by the Akkadian ruler Naram-Sin, and this destruction accidentally preserved the royal archive. However, the site does not appear to have been abandoned after this destruction; Ebla survived for another 600 years, and the city was rebuilt, although not the palace with the state archives. This new settlement was itself destroyed, in about 2000 BC, with clear signs of a fire. The city again appears to have been rebuilt on the destruction levels by the conquerors, without any break in occupation. Imposing city walls were erected in about 1900 BC. These enclosed the whole urban area and consisted of a massive earth embankment protected by plaster, and faced with dressed stone at the base. Many buildings were erected, including several temples and a large palace complex. The Lower City was still the residential zone. This city lasted until about 1600 BC, when the evidence again points to destruction by fire. This time the destruction was final and led to the abandonment of the site. Only sporadic occupation took place after that, mainly on the Acropolis, and only on the scale of a modest village; this occupation lasted right up to the Roman or Byzantine period, when there was a small community of monks. Apart from this settlement, Ebla has remained totally deserted.

VIJAYANAGARA, INDIA

The final destruction of many sites, like that at Ebla, leaves few standing ruins and little trace of the site above ground level, but at some sites, such as Vijayanagara, the attacking forces did not totally destroy the site, but left substantial ruins.

Vijayanagara, in the Krishna valley, is the best preserved Hindu royal site in southern

ABOVE *Vijayanagara was once one of the most magnificent capital cities in Asia, and by the mid 16th century it controlled almost all of the Hindu kingdoms in southern India.*

India. It is situated by the River Tungabhadra, and was founded in the 14th century. The Kingdom of Vijayanagara emerged as the most powerful military state in southern India at the end of the 12th century and remained so for over 200 years. By the mid-16th century it controlled almost all of the Hindu kingdoms in southern India. During this period, huge temple-cities emerged, and the ruins of Vijayanagara, one of these cities,

covered an area of 25sq.km (10sq. miles). It was one of the most magnificent capital cities in Asia, and its massive defensive walls enclosed administrative, residential and religious areas. To the north of the royal palace was a sacred settlement with temple complexes. The temples were responsible for land management and irrigation, with water being transported and stored by an elaborate system of tanks and canals. Trade flourished and there is evidence of trade both with the West and with China. The city was resplendent with temple towers, baths, fountains, pavilions, gardens and lakes. There were thousands of elephants, and the domed elephant stables, built of stone, still survive. Few other secular and domestic buildings were constructed of stone, and so little trace of them remains, but all around are the ruins of the many stone temples and royal buildings.

In 1565 Vijayanagara was attacked by the invading Muslim armies during the invasion of the subcontinent by the Mughals; the inhabitants escaped with as many of their goods and elephants as possible, and the site then became an abandoned ruin, although still a place of pilgrimage to this day.

....
LEFT *The stone temple chariot stands in the Vitthala temple at Vijayanagara in India, and is an example of the exquisite carving and immense labour used in the construction of the royal and religious buildings.*
....

....
RIGHT *Many royal and religious buildings constructed of stone survive at Vijayanagara (now called Hampi). Very few other buildings survive, as they were constructed of wood.*
....

ANGKOR, CAMBODIA

Angkor is another site where extensive ruins were completely abandoned after the place was attacked, but in this case the surrounding area became deserted as well, and the site was lost for several centuries.

In 1861, in the dense jungles of Cambodia, Henri Mouhot, a French naturalist, discovered enormous crumbling towers and temples, rising above a huge lake. They were inhabited only by a small community of Buddhist monks. These were the remains of Angkor (just north of the present town of Siem Reap), the once splendid capital of the Khmer kingdom, which for centuries had been abandoned to the swamps and jungle, but which has since been conserved and partly restored.

Angkor was situated by the Great Lake (Tonle Sap), and in the rainy season, the Mekong River flowed back into the lake, which then overflowed into the vast alluvial plain. The wealth of the Khmer kingdom depended on a highly sophisticated system of agriculture based on irrigation. A complex system was developed to take advantage of the water at the retreat of the floods in November, enabling rice and other crops to be cultivated. This supported a population of about one million people, and the empire became very rich, extending over much of south-east Asia. This system of agriculture continues to some extent today.

The group of sites collectively known as Angkor was established as the Khmer capital in about AD 881. The period from the 9th–14th century AD in south-east Asia was a time of powerful kingdoms. The Khmer kingdom adopted the Hindu religion from India, and major Hindu and Buddhist temple complexes were constructed throughout the region, influenced greatly by India.

From the 8th century, Jayavarman II instituted the philosophy of *Devaraja*, the worship of the god-king, whereby the Khmer kings attempted to create heaven on earth, and ruled by divine authority, to be worshipped and obeyed. This cult continued for several centuries. Angkor is more a replica of heaven than a centre of commerce, and in fact little evidence for domestic structures has yet been found. Another complex water management system was established, with vast reservoirs and canals for ritual purposes as well as for transporting stone for the construction of temples. The material excavated from the reservoirs and canals was also used to construct temple-mountains.

The Hindu temples were at first faced with brick and stone, but later ones were constructed almost wholly of sandstone. Using slave labour, over 250 monuments were constructed, which were intended to represent mountains, the ideal place to make contact with the gods. Each Khmer king had a temple built, trying to surpass his predecessor. The huge temples basically consisted of a rectangular walled enclosure, with an artificial "mountain" rising in terraces, and a shrine on the top terrace. The temples were often adorned with relief sculptures, which provide much information

RIGHT *The Bayon temple was constructed within the Angkor Thom walled city in about AD 1200, and required huge quantities of stone. It has 54 towers rising to a height of 45 m (148 ft). Earlier parts of the city had to be destroyed for the construction of Angkor Thom and its Bayon temple.*

on the spiritual and everyday life at Angkor. The buildings were immense feats of engineering, and yet these builders did not know how to construct the "true arch".

The first temple to be constructed was the Bakong (AD 881), followed by a whole series which culminated in the largest temple complex, Angkor Wat. This was built in the early 12th century by Suryavarman II, and measures 1550 x 1400m (1700 × 1500yd), and has over 1.6km (1 mile) of sculpture. Angkor Wat took about 25 years to build and is believed to be the largest religious structure in the world. It is a 3-storied pyramid topped by five towers, which symbolize the five peaks of Mount Meru, the dwelling place of the gods in Hindu cosmology.

In its heyday, the Angkor complex stretched more than 25km (15 miles) east-west and nearly 10 km (6 miles) north-south. The Khmer kingdom then appears to have weakened and suffered a series of foreign attacks and internal conflicts. After Suryavarman II died, the neighbouring people of Champa successfully seized Angkor and sacked it in 1177. They were later repulsed, but no more great Hindu shrines were built in Angkor. There was a brief revival of Angkor's splendour under Jayavarman VII (1181–c.1215), who adopted Buddhism as the state religion, and restored the fortunes of the Khmer kingdom. During his reign the walled city of Angkor Thom was constructed, including the Bayon temple. Angkor Thom contained more stone than all the Egyptian pyramids together! It was surrounded by extensive moats and walls.

LEFT *The early 12th century temple complex of Angkor Wat, Cambodia, as viewed across one of the vast artificially constructed reservoirs. The five towers on top of this three-storey pyramid represent the five peaks of Mount Meru, believed to be the dwelling place of the gods.*

The Bayon temple has 54 towers rising to a height of about 45m (150ft), but unlike other temples, it had no surrounding moat or wall.

After this, though, the Khmer kingdom became impoverished and Angkor declined. In the 13th century the water management system broke down, although agricultural irrigation continued. Repeated attacks by the warlike Siamese weakened the empire and it gradually broke up. The great temples fell into decline by the later 13th century, and in the 15th century, the Khmer kingdom collapsed when control of the manpower could no longer be maintained. Angkor was attacked and besieged by the Siamese in 1431, and was ransacked and devastated. Returning to the site the following year, the Siamese found the vast capital inexplicably abandoned: the remaining population had vanished, leaving the palaces and temples to be reclaimed by the jungle. Angkor eventually passed into legend as a lost city.

SAN LORENZO, MEXICO

When a site is destroyed and abandoned, and there are no written records to tell exactly what happened, it is not always possible to obtain a clear picture from the archaeological evidence alone. In the case of San Lorenzo, for example, it is not certain whether attack by invaders or whether internal strife was responsible for the destruction and abandonment of the site.

Between 1200 BC and 300 BC simple village societies in Mesoamerica developed into urban civilizations. The most well-known

culture of this period is that of the Olmec, whose homeland lay in an area of some 200 x 50km (125 × 30 miles) in the wet tropical forests of southern Veracruz and Tabasco, on the coast of the Gulf of Mexico. The Olmec is the earliest civilization in Mexico, and its influence spread throughout much of Mesoamerica. It is particularly noted for its ceremonial centres and its distinctive art style, including colossal stone heads (never with bodies). Were-jaguars (a combination of a snarling jaguar and a weeping human infant) were also part of the art style.

The earliest of the Olmec ceremonial centres was San Lorenzo, situated 80km (50 miles) inland, near a branch of the Coatzacoalos River in southern Veracruz. The site was on a natural plateau, about 50m (160ft) above the surrounding lowland and measuring 1.25km (0.8 miles) north-south. The upper 7m (23ft) of the site was an artificial mound formed from earth and clay, with a series of human-made ravines and ridges, which may not have been completed. The site flourished from 1200 BC to 900 BC. It was discovered in 1945, and between 1966 and 1968 San Lorenzo was excavated by an expedition from Yale University.

The main feature on the summit of the plateau, the immense artificially raised platform, had ceremonial courtyards, including pools for ritual bathing and an earthen court for a ceremonial ball game, which eventually spread over much of America and had a ritual significance. There were also more than 200 house mounds, with evidence from excavations that the community was supported by agriculture in the surrounding area. The predominant crop was maize, and the local diet included fish and dogs, with occasional deer and wild pig. There is also evidence for cannibalism. Thousands of obsidian artefacts have been found. The obsidian was imported from Mexico and Guatemala, indicating extensive trading networks. Many other domestic remains including pottery were also recovered in the excavations.

Excess water from the ceremonial pools was removed through an elaborate network of deeply buried U-shaped basalt drains with covers. The basalt was brought from the Tuxtla Mountains, a distance of 80km (50 miles). Of particular note are some sixty monuments, also of basalt, including *stelae* (tall slab-like monuments), reliefs, columns, and eight colossal heads of rulers up to 2.85m (9ft) high and weighing 25 tonnes, all carved without metal tools. There were also large flat-topped basalt blocks with carvings which were possibly used as thrones or altars, weighing up to 40 tonnes. The powerful art style in these monumental carvings based on part human, part animal figures gives an insight into the religion.

In about 900 BC the site was destroyed, but it is not clear if this was done through invasion, political revolution, or even for ritual reasons. The monuments were smashed and defaced and were buried in rows along the tops of the ridges, and some of them eventually tumbled into the ravines. The site was re-occupied after a short period of abandonment, but was totally deserted by 400 BC.

LEFT *The Olmec style of art is very distinctive, particularly the stylized colossal stone heads, never carved with bodies. Olmec influence spread throughout much of Mesoamerica, and this head was found at Guadalajara in Mexico.*

LA VENTA, MEXICO

The site at La Venta is closely connected with San Lorenzo. This site, in Tabasco province, flourished from 1000 BC to 600 BC, but grew in importance after the destruction of San Lorenzo in 900 BC. La Venta was one of the greatest Olmec sites, a large ceremonial centre located on an island in the swampy wastes of the lower Tonalá River. It was about 18km (11 miles) from the coast, and had no nearby farmland or building stone sources. The site has now been largely destroyed by oil operations, and the huge carvings from the site have been set up in a park named La Venta in Villahermosa, and is an outdoor museum.

The site was dominated by a massive 34m (112ft) high mound or pyramid of clay. There was a complex of other low platform mounds, which may have supported elite settlements, and also courtyards, all spread over a distance of some 2.5km (1.6 miles). One courtyard had a palisade of monolithic basalt columns, each over 2m (6ft) tall. The site is best known for its stone sculptures, the stone being brought from over 100km (60 miles) away.

These consisted of carved stelae, altars, four colossal heads, and three rectangular pavements made of blocks of serpentine laid in the form of jaguar masks. There is also evidence for long-distance trade in jade. A number of buried offerings has been found at La Venta, including one notable find of the burial of 16 stone figurines and 6 axes arranged in a circular setting, obviously representing a ritual scene. The carved figurines were 18cm (7in) high and were made of jade, serpentine and granite.

Domestic finds from the site have been very sparse, and only a few burials have been found, although these had very rich grave goods.

Like San Lorenzo centuries before, La Venta was defaced, violently destroyed and abandoned in about 400–300 BC, bringing to an end the heyday of the Olmec civilization.

TEOTIHUACÁN, MEXICO

Teotihuacán is another site where the circumstances of its destruction are not entirely clear. It is one of the most important prehistoric sites in Mexico, and is situated in the Valley of Mexico, 40km (25 miles) north of Mexico City. Teotihuacán was first inhabited from about 150 BC, but the first ceremonial buildings were constructed in the 1st-2nd centuries AD. In the 1st century AD,

ABOVE *Little massive stone sculpture is found at Teotihuacán in Mexico, except as architectural embellishment. There are, however, hundreds of painted murals. In the later life of the city, warriors appear more and more as subjects in art, coinciding with the decline in the city, ending with its destruction around AD 750.*

RIGHT *The Pyramid of the Moon was at one end of the 5-km-(3-mile-) long Avenue of the Dead at Teotihuacán, Mexico, and was probably constructed in the 1st-2nd century AD. The whole city was laid out at this time on a regular grid, never before seen in the New World, and the city reached its peak between AD 400 and 600.*

the city was laid out in a grid pattern. It became what was probably the largest urban centre in Mesoamerica, and reached its peak between AD 400–600, when there may have been a population of 200,000. Teotihuacán was then the sixth largest city in the world, directly controlling a large area of central Mexico, and having influence over an even greater area (which is particularly evident in the art and architecture of distant sites). There are no written records, and so the hierarchical structure is not known, but there must have been a powerful ruling class. It is not at all certain who the people of Teotihuacán were.

The city covered an area of over 23sq.km (9sq. miles), and has been mapped by René Millon using *photogrammetry*, in a project lasting many years. The site was a very important centre of pilgrimage, and hundreds of temples and altars have been identified. At the heart of the city was the ceremonial complex which consisted of more than 100 shrines and pyramids grouped round the central north-south roadway known as the Avenue of the Dead. The Pyramids of the Sun and the Moon are immense; the former is 70m (230ft) high and was constructed from an estimated million cubic metres (over a million cubic yards) of sun-dried brick and rubble. It was built over a cave, which itself was probably an earlier cult centre. Many of Teotihuacán's buildings were constructed with sun-dried bricks and stones coated with lime plaster.

At the intersection of the Avenue of the Dead and the main east-west axis are the Great Compound and the Ciudadela. The Great Compound may have been the central marketplace, and the Ciudadela was a vast complex forming the political, religious, administrative and military centre of the city. The rulers probably lived in palaces within the Ciudadela. Within the rest of the city, over 500 craft workshops have been identified, many making pottery or objects of obsidian, and Teotihuacán seems to have controlled the trade in, and sources of obsidian. Near the western edge of the city was a zone occupied by foreigners from Oaxaca, and on the east by the Maya. Other inhabitants lived in single-storey rectangular compounds, of which over 20,000 have been recognized, while others lived in what may have been slum dwellings.

Apart from some architectural features, there is little in the way of stone carving, but there are hundreds of painted murals. Between AD 650 and 750 warriors appear increasingly as subjects in art, and from about AD 650 the city began to decline and the population decreased. In about AD 750 the city was destroyed through burning and deliberate destruction, and must have been sacked. The reason for its destruction and abandonment is not known, since there is no good reason to suggest a foreign invasion. It has been suggested that over-exploitation of resources including the destruction of forests, particularly for lime burning, led to erosion and dessication of the land; the resulting collapse of agriculture may have weakened the state, leading to outside invasion. The city was never rebuilt, although some of the

RIGHT *The well-preserved Hellenistic temple at Hatra in Iraq was constructed in the 1st century BC. It was set on a podium, and was surrounded by a double colonnade.*

ruins continued to be inhabited by squatters for 100 years or more. The Aztecs gradually assumed power in Mexico, and Teotihuacan remained a place of pilgrimage until the downfall of the Aztecs in 1521.

HATRA, IRAQ

Where a place has been sacked and destroyed, the archaeological evidence does not always make it possible to distinguish between attack by foreign invaders and internal insurrection. It is only where written records exist, as for Hatra, that it is certain that the destruction represents an attack by alien invaders.

Hatra (present-day al-Hadr) lies 100km (60 miles) south of Mosul on the west bank of the Wadi Tharthar. It lies in the desert between the Tigris and the Euphrates, and was a strongly fortified oasis settlement. It probably came into existence in the 1st century BC as one of the earliest settlements of Arabic-speaking nomad tribes. The area between the Tigris and Euphrates became a province of the Parthian empire, called Arabaya or "Land of the Arabs", and Hatra flourished as the capital of this satellite kingdom, under Arab rulers. These rulers first of all had the title of lords or chiefs, and then later kings. Hatra acted as a caravan city fortified to withstand the invading Roman armies. The city successfully held out against several attempts by the Romans to take it under the emperors Trajan and Septimius Severus (in AD 117 and 198-201). After the fall of the Parthians and the rise of the Sassanians,

LEFT *The central part of the city at Hatra has many temples with contrasting architectural styles. On the right is the Hellenistic-style temple, a style of architecture current at Hatra through the 1st century BC. In the 1st century AD a temple complex was built on the left in the later Iranian style.*

BELOW *The city walls at Hatra in Iraq were built of mud brick and limestone. This roadway leads from a gateway in the walls across the city (once with numerous dwelling houses) to the central enclosure.*

ABOVE *From the 1st century BC, Hatra in Iraq was a flourishing caravan city in the midst of the desert between the Tigris and Euphrates. Several temples were constructed in the central enclosure, including a well-preserved Hellenistic temple.*

Hatra became allied with Rome, but in AD 240 it was abandoned after being destroyed by the Sassanian king Ardashir and his son Shapur I. From Arabic inscriptions it seems that there was brief reoccupation of the site in the 12th century.

Hatra's prosperity seems to have been based on being a cosmopolitan trading centre. There is also evidence of numerous deities worshipped by the people of the various nomad tribes who came to the city. Some remarkable ruins of the Parthian period survive, and excavations of some of these took place in the 1970s. The buildings are of mud brick and limestone, and include the city walls and gates, houses and tombs. There is also a partly restored temple in the Hellenistic style of architecture, a style current at Hatra until the 1st century BC, and a temple complex in the later Iranian style of the 1st century AD. This latter temple has two main units, each with a great open-ended hall or *iwan*, flanked by smaller iwans and other vaulted chambers. Many stone statues have been recovered and are now in the Mosul and Baghdad museums, as well as numerous inscriptions.

NIMRUD, IRAQ

Another well-documented site that was attacked and destroyed by foreign armies is that of Nimrud, the site of ancient Kalhu (biblical Calah). It is situated between Nineveh and the River Zab, on the east bank of the River Tigris, 31km (20 miles) south of Mosul. The River Tigris once flowed beneath

its walls but has since moved half a mile (one kilometre) away, although the ancient bed of the river is still visible. The site was excavated last century by Layard, and subsequently by Sir Max Mallowan, and again more recently.

There was some early occupation of the site from the 3rd millenium BC, but a town was founded on the site by Shalmaneser I of Assyria in the mid-13th century BC. The capital at that time was at Assur, but in about 880 BC, Assurnasirpal II (884–859 BC) moved the capital to Nimrud, a more central position in relation to the Assyrian empire. The city was refounded and considerably enlarged. The mud brick city walls were rebuilt and extended, enclosing an enlarged rectangular area of about 350 hectares (870 acres). The

....
ABOVE *The extensive site of Nimrud in Iraq has undergone several excavations and some restoration. This view of the citadel is looking south towards the 20m- (66ft-) high ziggurat in the distance. Much of the citadel was occupied by temples and palaces. In the foreground is the largest temple, dedicated to Nabu, the god of writing.*
....
OPPOSITE PAGE
Numerous bas-reliefs, sculptures and inscriptions have been found at Nimrud in Iraq.
....

king also constructed a canal from the River Zab to provide irrigation for the gardens of the royal city. The city walls were bordered on the west by the old course of the River Tigris and on the south by a wide canal.

Much of Nimrud remains unexplored. The city consisted mainly of the houses of the inhabitants; a population of some 80,000 people, judging by some of the inscriptions found. The citadel in the south-west was crowned by a *ziggurat* 20m (66ft) high, and inside the citadel were successive palaces and temples built by Assyrian monarchs. The Northwest palace inside the citadel was a huge complex built by Assurnasirpal II, and was the first Assyrian building to be embellished by massive stone bas-reliefs and

escape the clouds of gas. About 2000 people were killed – a tenth of the population. Earthquake shocks accompanying the eruption destroyed many buildings and the whole city was buried by a layer of ash and stones up to 4m (13ft) deep.

The survivors did not attempt rebuilding, but tried to salvage and loot as much as possible by sinking tunnels, sometimes cutting through walls of buildings in the process. After this the site was abandoned and effectively lost, although the existence of the site was still known, because of references to the disaster in Roman literature, and in particular in letters of Pliny the Younger to Tacitus, which give an eye-witness account of the eruption. The exact site of the city was rediscovered in the middle of the 18th century, when tunnelling took place to plunder objects from the site. Excavation began in earnest in 1860 and has continued until recently. Three-fifths of the

....
LEFT *The whole Roman city of Pompeii in Italy was buried in the volcanic eruption to a depth of 4 m (13 ft), so the city was not rebuilt. About three-fifths of the site have been excavated.*
....
ABOVE *A wall painting of the mid 1st century AD from Pompeii, in Italy, showing the head of a*

young girl with a book and pen, in a contemplative mood.
....
BELOW *A plaster cast of the body of a young woman who did not escape the volcanic eruption at Pompeii, in Italy, in AD 79, but died of suffocation.*
....

chapter four

Disaster

The most dramatic of all the reasons why places are abandoned are the sudden natural disasters, such as earthquakes, tornadoes, avalanches and volcanic eruptions. In many cases the survivors of the disaster begin clearing a site and rebuilding soon after, but sometimes this has not happened. Some places were just abandoned, perhaps because rebuilding was impossible because of the lack of resources needed to rebuild, or for reasons now lost to us. These sites are very important for archaeology because they often provide a collection of evidence that is uncontaminated by later occupation – a "time capsule". Often, too, a disaster can wreck a site or region so badly that it has to be abandoned, but it is remembered for many years; much is talked and written about these disasters so that we may know the exact year, and even the actual day and time when it occurred. Such is the case with the cities of Pompeii and Herculaneum.

POMPEII, ITALY

The origin of the city of Pompeii is obscure. It lies on the Bay of Naples in south-west Italy, and there is evidence of early Greek and Etruscan influence, but the town was taken over by the Samnite tribes around 420 BC. It remained a Samnite town of Oscan-speaking inhabitants until it was besieged and captured by Sulla in 89 BC. In 80 BC a colony of war veterans was established at Pompeii, and this brought rapid Romanization, enhanced status and wealth, as well as villas in the surrounding countryside. The town prospered for over a hundred years until a violent earthquake nearly destroyed the town in AD 62. Despite widespread damage, large-scale rebuilding was put in hand, some of which was still incomplete when the city was engulfed during the volcanic eruption in AD 79.

Serious volcanic activity from Vesuvius, which lay about 10km (6 miles) to the north of the city, had not occurred within living memory, and it seems that many inhabitants did not realise the danger until it was too late. On the morning of 24th August, in AD 79, Vesuvius erupted, giving off a great cloud of hot ash and poisonous gases. Many people stayed indoors sheltering from the rain of hot stones and ashes until it was too late to

BELOW *Many rooms in the palaces at Nimrud in Iraq were filled with ivory objects, including delicately carved plaques. This example still has traces of decorative coloured paste.*

WOLSTENHOLME TOWNE, MARTIN'S HUNDRED, UNITED STATES OF AMERICA

Occasionally, where a site was occupied for only a short time before it was attacked and destroyed, it can act as a "time capsule", providing archaeologists with a range of closely-dated evidence, free from the contamination caused by being mixed with artefacts of different dates. One such site is Wolstenholme Towne in Virginia, close to Williamsburg and 16km (10 miles) east of Jamestown; it was only occupied for a few years before it was attacked, destroyed and abandoned.

Wolstenholme Towne was the central town of Martin's Hundred, a plantation of over 20,000 acres, and one of many private British plantations established in the early 17th century. The colony at Wolstenholme Towne was established in 1619 on the James River by about 200 settlers. In 1622 the colonists provoked a major Indian attack, and the settlement was destroyed on March 22. A few survivors and some new settlers tried to rebuild the site, but disease took its toll, and the site was abandoned and long forgotten. Part of it has probably been washed away by the James River. Nevertheless, some surviving historical documents have been able to shed some light on the settlement and its inhabitants.

The site was discovered in 1970 by archaeologists searching for signs of the later 18th century plantation of Carter's Grove. Unexpectedly, evidence of a much earlier occupation was found, including the settlement at Wolstenholme Towne. Excavation of the site began in 1977, and has revealed information about dwellings, storehouses, and a timber fort. It is thought to be the earliest colonial settlement yet uncovered in North America, and was built on the same pattern as similar settlements of that period in northern Ireland.

Many British and European artefacts of the 17th century have been found, brought to their new country by the colonists, and these include pottery, weapons and armour (such as rare finds of iron helmets), agricultural implements, and many domestic items. The graves of massacred colonists and charred remains have also been found, indicating the tragic nature of the colony's end.

RIGHT One of a pair of ivory plaques depicting a lioness killing her victim amongst lotus and papyrus plants. Found deep in a well at Nimrud. The plaques may have been the work of a Phoenician craftsman, imported to decorate the throne of King Sargon (721–705 BC). They had carnelian and lapis lazuli insets.

RIGHT Giant guardian figures and bas-reliefs at the gateway of the Northwest palace at Nimrud in Iraq. The figures are winged human-headed lions, and were carved from limestone. They are 3.5 m (11½ ft) high and date to the 9th century BC.

giant guardian figures (winged lions and bulls) at the gateways. Many of these monumental sculptures were brought back to England by Layard and are now in the British Museum. This palace was also a treasure house, audience chamber and administrative centre.

In the south-east corner of the city, Shalmaneser III (859-824 BC) built a huge arsenal-palace, with military barracks, workshops, stores, palace and treasure-house. Many rooms were filled with ivory objects and cuneiform tablets. Numerous ivory objects, including delicately carved plaques, have been found at Nimrud, many of which were collected along with other valuable goods as tribute by the kings.

In the late 8th century (c. 710 BC), the capital was moved by Sargon II (721–705 BC) to Khorsabad and then to Nineveh. The Assyrian empire gradually weakened and suffered internal strife, and at the end of the 7th century BC, Assyria's enemies joined forces to overthrow the empire. In 614 BC Assur was sacked and burned by a Median army in collaboration with the Babylonians, and in 612 BC Nineveh and Nimrud were sacked and destroyed, with evidence for burning being found from excavations. In Fort Shalmaneser a mass burial of people killed in the final sack of 612 BC has been found. A few survivors remained at Nimrud, but the site was deserted by the time Xenophon passed by in 401 BC and recorded a description. The Tigris had by then shifted 3km (2 miles) to the west. A Hellenistic village grew up on the ruined citadel, but this too was abandoned in about 150 BC.

HERCULANEUM, ITALY

The eruption that destroyed Pompeii affected much of the countryside around Vesuvius, destroying many small farming settlements and villas. It also completely buried another Roman coastal town – Herculaneum. Herculaneum was a small, wealthy town situated, like Pompeii, on the coast of south-west Italy. This town, 8km (5 miles) from Naples, also suffered damage in the earthquake that wrecked Pompeii in AD 62, but as at Pompeii, it was repaired and rebuilt.

The origin of the town is not clear. It may have been a Greek settlement, or an Oscan town with a Greek trading centre added to it. As with many settlements in the area, the early town also shows evidence of Etruscan and Samnite influence. It became a Roman town in 89 BC.

Pompeii lay to the south of Vesuvius and was engulfed by falling ash and stones, but Herculaneum is situated at the bottom of the western slopes of the volcano and was buried by a flow of liquid mud, which reached a depth of over 20m (66ft) in some areas. The mud completely obliterated the town and solidified, and it is probably because of the depth of the mud that there was little

LEFT *A mosaic from Herculaneum, in the House of Neptune and Amphitrite.*

RIGHT *The public baths at Herculaneum in Italy would have been an important focus of social life.*

attempt at salvage or looting after the disaster. The location of the town was lost until the 18th century, and excavations began soon after its discovery. The early excavations were shafts and tunnels because of the great depth of overlying deposits, and these excavations formed a warren of underground passages by which visitors could view the remains. In the 19th century and in modern excavations a substantial part of the town has been cleared of the volcanic mud, but large areas are still unexcavated.

Traces of people killed during the disaster are much rarer at Herculaneum than at Pompeii. This is due in part to the fact that Herculaneum was much smaller and its population was perhaps a quarter of that at Pompeii. Also, being closer to the volcano, the inhabitants would have been more aware of the danger and probably fled the city while the mud was still covering the surrounding villages and farms, and had not reached the town itself.

Like Pompeii, Herculaneum provides an example of a flourishing Roman town in the year AD 79, but the example from Herculaneum is much more complete. Because the depth of covering deposits discouraged looting, more artefacts have survived, but of much greater importance is the fact that the hot volcanic mud had the property of preserving organic remains, so that wooden doors, furniture and other objects survived. Excavations have recovered fabrics, rolls of papyrus, and even food – food stored in shops and kitchens, and the remains of meals hastily abandoned as the people fled.

ABOVE *When a disaster occurs, the surviving inhabitants often rebuild their settlement on the same site if that is possible. On the island of Santorini in Greece, modern buildings have been constructed on or near those destroyed in successive earthquakes. Beneath the town can be seen volcanic deposits relating to the destruction and burial of the Bronze Age settlement of Akrotiri.*

LEFT *The survival at Herculaneum is often better than that at Pompeii, and many organic remains were preserved, such as wooden doors and furniture.*

AKROTIRI, SANTORINI, GREECE

It is not always the case, though, that ancient disasters are so well documented that knowledge of them survives to the present day. Some sites totally destroyed or overwhelmed by volcanic debris have lain undetected for centuries and have then been discovered by chance. One such site is Akrotiri.

The town of Akrotiri is situated in the south of the main island of Thera (also known as Santorini), which lies in the Aegean Sea, about 100km (62 miles) north of Crete. During the Bronze Age, this town was a thriving settlement which had strong connections with the Minoan civilization on Crete, but around 1500 BC the town was abandoned because of an earthquake, and was

subsequently buried by volcanic ash.

The island of Thera, on which Akrotiri lies, is a volcano. The volcanic activity that gave rise to the earthquake, causing Akrotiri to be evacuated, was followed by a massive volcanic eruption which may have been several times greater than the eruption that destroyed Krakatoa in 1883. The eruption blew the centre out of the island of Thera, burying Akrotiri under volcanic ash 30m (100ft) deep, and creating clouds of ash and seismic flood waves in the surrounding area. The damage on Crete caused by earthquake, flood waves and falling volcanic ash, which almost certainly caused a disruption of agriculture for some years, probably made eastern Crete virtually uninhabitable for a time and may have been the ultimate factor that led to the collapse of the Minoan civilization in about 1200 BC.

We do not yet know the exact dates of the earthquake and subsequent volcanic eruption, but it seems clear that Akrotiri was abandoned before the end of the Minoan civilization. It has been suggested that at the time of the earthquake, Akrotiri was partially buried by ash, but a few buildings appear to have been reoccupied, only to be hastily abandoned during the later eruption. The exact time lapse between the earthquake and the volcanic explosion may be anything up to 50 years, but it is more likely to have been a shorter period.

The fall of ash completely obliterated Akrotiri, and the site was unknown until there were chance finds of the remains of buildings in the late 19th century.

....
LEFT *The Bronze Age settlement at Akrotiri on the island of Santorini was first of all destroyed by an earthquake and then by a huge volcanic eruption, which totally buried all trace of this past civilisation. The site was only found by chance in the late 19th century.*
....

....
ABOVE *Preservation of buildings at Akrotiri, on Santorini, is extremely good, with painted frescoes surviving in some rooms, and numerous objects left just as they were abandoned. These large pottery jars (right) would have been used for the storage of food.*
....

ABOVE *Before its destruction and abandonment in 1793, Cowdray House in England was an imposing Tudor mansion built round a large quadrangular courtyard. This is part of the east wing, with the north-east hexagonal tower. On the left the north wing has been demolished.*

RIGHT *On 7th September 1793 Cowdray House in England was gutted by fire, just a week before the eighth Viscount Montague was drowned in a boating accident. These two disasters fulfilled a legendary curse laid on the owners of the house some 250 years earlier.*

A campaign of excavations was conducted from 1967 to 1974 by Professor S. Marinatos, but he was killed on the site in 1974, when an ancient wall collapsed. He is buried in a grave in one of the houses that he excavated. His excavations have revealed just how important the site is, and a larger area of the site has been uncovered in subsequent excavations.

Because the volcanic ash covering Akrotiri compacted to form soft rock, the preservation of the remains is surprisingly good, with some buildings surviving two and three storeys high. Some rooms have painted frescoes, and pottery, various types of artefact, and even identifiable food remains have been preserved in the positions they occupied when they were abandoned.

COWDRAY HOUSE, ENGLAND

Although disasters, such as the burial of Akrotiri under thousands of tons of ash and rock, may preserve spectacular remains for archaeologists to uncover many centuries later, such disasters are relatively infrequent. Much more common are disasters caused by fire, earth and water. Sites are burned down, flooded or buried by landslips every year, but in most cases such sites are repaired or rebuilt. Even after the Great Fire of London in 1666, which devastated an area of over 160 hectares (400 acres), destroying 13,200 houses and 89 churches, rebuilding of the city began immediately. Sometimes, though, such destruction leads to abandonment, as in the case of Cowdray ruins in Sussex.

The lords of the manor of Midhurst and Easebourne, from the 1180s until the 16th century, were the Bohun family. In about 1273 the family moved to a new house. It was surrounded by a moat on low ground, near the River Rother. In the 1520s this house was demolished, and on the same site a new house – Cowdray House – was built. It took sixty years to build under three owners. In 1529 the estate changed hands and passed to Sir William Fitzwilliam. In 1542 it passed to Sir Anthony Browne, and then in 1554, to his son (also called Sir Anthony Browne) who became the first Viscount Montague. Apart from being seized by the Commonwealth between 1643 and 1660, because the third Viscount had favoured the losing side in the Civil War, the estate remained in the possession of the Browne family until the last of the line, the eighth Viscount Montague,

....
ABOVE *After its destruction by fire, the Tudor mansion at Cowdray in England was never lived in again, and some of it had to be pulled down as it was potentially dangerous. This is part of the surviving hexagonal north-east tower, with its fine set of chimney stacks.*
....

was drowned in a boating accident on the Rhine. Unknown to him, a week before his death Cowdray House and its contents had been completely destroyed.

On the night of 7th September 1793 the whole house was gutted by fire. Cowdray was never lived in again. Ironically, alteration and redecoration of part of the house were being carried out in expectation of the eighth Viscount's return from the Continent, and it is thought that an unattended fire left by the workmen was the cause of the blaze. The ruins of the building were neglected for over a hundred years and much of it had to be pulled down because of its dangerous state. Early this century the remaining ruins were made wind and weather proof to prevent further decay.

Legend has it that the owners of Cowdray House were cursed, and the disaster was the result of this. The first Sir Anthony Browne gained much of his wealth at the time of the Dissolution of the Monasteries. He inherited the estate of Easebourne Priory from his half-brother, Sir William Fitzwilliam, who died childless. The sub-prioress of Easebourne, when evicted from the Priory, was supposed to have called down the curse of Heaven in fire and water on whoever was given Easebourne Priory, and on his male descendants. Sir Anthony himself was given Battle Abbey near Hastings where legend says that the Abbot (or, in some versions, the ghost of a monk) cursed Sir Anthony, predicting that his name would be wiped from the land by fire and water. The disastrous fire some 250 years later, coinciding

as it did with the death of the last male descendant of Sir Anthony by drowning, inevitably caused the superstitious to connect the events with the legendary curses on the family.

Before its destruction and abandonment, Cowdray was an imposing Tudor mansion, built mainly of brick. It was arranged round a large quadrangular courtyard, although the north and south wings have now been demolished down to their foundations. The original building contained a great hall, chapel, and a hexagonal tower containing the kitchen; the latter tower was the only part to escape the fire.

Between 1535 and 1542 various additions were made to the house in order to complete it, including a gatehouse, a hexagonal tower, and embattlements which gave the mansion the appearance of a fortified castle. In the first half of the 18th century considerable alterations were done to the house, including the enlargement of many windows and doors. Today all that is left of this once magnificent house are the picturesque ruins alongside the River Rother, just north-east of Midhurst.

PORT ROYAL, JAMAICA

Fire has always been a common cause of destruction, and on occasion, abandonment of sites. But where sites are devastated by flooding or landslip they may remain uninhabitable for some time, forcing them to be abandoned. One such site is Port Royal in Jamaica.

ABOVE *An aerial view of Port Royal, Jamaica, as it is today on the spit at the mouth of Kingston Harbour. Much of the 17th-century town was destroyed by an earthquake in 1692 and sank into the sea.*

OPPOSITE *A view across the quadrangle towards the west wing of Cowdray House, England, with its imposing tall and narrow gatehouse. The gatehouse has four polygonal battlemented turrets, and was built between 1535 and 1542 by Sir William Fitzwilliam.*

In 1655 the island of Jamaica was captured by the English in an attempt to break the Spanish monopoly of the trade routes in the Caribbean. On the south coast the town of Port Royal was established by Oliver Cromwell's soldiers. It rapidly grew in size and became rich as the most important trading centre in the Caribbean and by preying on Spanish shipping. It was known as "the most wicked city in the world" from its association with the buccaneers and pirates that used the port. By 1692 there were 8000 inhabitants. On 7th June 1692 a powerful earthquake that lasted three minutes almost totally destroyed Port Royal, and only an inner nucleus of streets survived above water. The seaward part of the town, an area

ABOVE *Port Royal's main standing monument is Fort Charles, built originally to guard the entrance to Kingston Harbour. This part of the town did not fall into the sea in the earthquake of 1692, probably thanks to the underlying geology. Sites such as this and the evidence from excavations are being used to develop tourism.*

LEFT *Port Royal's 18th- and 19th-century dockyard is now overgrown and disused.*

of 8 hectares (20 acres), sank into deep water, never to be reclaimed.

In the 18th and 19th centuries Port Royal was rebuilt as a naval dockyard, and early in his career Horatio Nelson is known to have served there for a time. Even after the earthquake of 1692, Port Royal suffered further earthquakes, principally in 1907, as well as fires and hurricanes. The military settlement was subsequently abandoned in 1907, and the dockyard became disused and overgrown.

Port Royal is now a small fishing village, but plans are in hand to develop the historic site as a focus for tourism. Much of the 17th century town still lies intact beneath the ground, although damaged by the earthquake, and a great deal survives 5m (15ft) underwater. Archaeological work has taken place in recent years, both on land and underwater, using modern survey and excavation techniques. Excavation on land has revealed a succession of well-preserved and identifiable deposits dating from the 17th century, particularly in the later dockyard area, where much land was reclaimed during the 18th century. An old abandoned church belonging to the original town of Port Royal was found in an excavation carried out in 1969. It was 2m (6ft) below ground, but still had evidence of its pews surviving.

The preservation of the 17th century town surviving underwater is also extremely good. With the aid of old maps and echo-sounding equipment, the position of the vanished forts and other buildings is being plotted. Some excavation has also taken

ABOVE *Trial excavations by the Jamaica National Heritage Trust and a team of British specialists on a site in Lime Street, Port Royal, in 1988. Here the foundations of 18th-century buildings are being recorded by methods developed in London.*

place, and a variety of objects from the site has been found including cannons, cannon balls, various utensils, candlesticks, clay pipes, tableware, expensive glassware, and hundreds of wine bottles. Many of the objects originally came from Britain and other parts of Europe, and provide a vivid picture of 17th century English colonial life.

chapter five

Market Forces

The abandonment of many places has been brought about by various changes in social conditions. Often it is a combination of political, religious and economic forces that leads to the abandonment of a site, although there is usually one single dominating factor that finally results in the desertion of a site.

EL-AMARNA, EGYPT

In the case of el-Amarna in Egypt, it was the adoption and rejection of a new religion that led to the founding and subsequent abandonment of the city of el-Amarna. In about 1370 BC, towards the end of the 18th Dynasty, King Amenophis IV introduced the monotheistic cult of Aten, the Sun God (represented by the sun's disk), setting aside the worship of the traditional gods of ancient Egypt. At the same time he changed his name to Akhenaten. The king moved his capital from Thebes to a fresh site along the Nile, midway between Memphis and Thebes. Here a completely new city was built called Akhetaten, today known as Amarna, el-Amarna or Tell el-Amarna. It is situated in a somewhat unattractive area, prone to

flooding from the occasional downpours. The city stretches for some 6km (3.5 miles) along the Nile, about 1km (0.6 miles) inland from the river bank, and is encircled by cliffs.

El-Amarna was divided into zones, with a comparatively remote royal residence in the north and with other areas containing the main temples, a ceremonial palace and administrative quarters. The city was constructed almost entirely of mud brick, although some stone was used, particularly for the temples. The king planned for himself and his courtiers to be buried in rock-cut tombs in the surrounding cliffs, which flouted the tradition of burying the dead on the west bank of the Nile, but only the tomb of Akhenaten was ever finished. Fourteen large stone stelae still survive which were set up to mark the boundaries of the city.

In order to house the workforce needed to build the city and the tombs, there was also a purpose-built village situated between the cliffs and the South City. The houses were constructed mainly of wood and brick, with painted walls and ceilings. There were no wells, and so water had to be brought from the river 3km (2 miles) away. Excavations

LEFT *El Deir, "the monastery", is one of the largest and finest rock-cut tombs in Petra, and was probably constructed in the 1st century AD. The doorway to the temple is 8 m high and leads to a large rock-cut chamber.*

have revealed that some of the labour force continued to worship the old gods instead of observing the newly adopted monotheistic cult of Aten.

The king Akhenaten was regarded as a heretic, and soon after his death there was a restoration of traditional religious beliefs. The city was deliberately abandoned by his successor Tutankhamen, along with Amarna village. The court returned to Thebes, while the labour force once again went back to live in the village of Deir el-Medina. Some of the stone buildings at Amarna were demolished so that the stone could be used elsewhere,

LEFT *El-Amarna is today a featureless desert site, but it was the capital of Egypt from about 1370 to 1350 BC. The city was found by chance in 1888, and remains a time capsule because it was inhabited for such a short time.*

BOTTOM LEFT A *relief sculpture of King Akhenaten under the rays of the sun god Aten, from el-Amarna, Egypt.*

BELOW Many *fascinating discoveries have been found at el-Amarna in Egypt, including the royal archive with a huge collection of clay tablets. Evidence of fairly large-scale glass working was also found in excavations conducted by Flinders Petrie. This selection shows fragmentary objects and scrap glass (cullet) from the site.*

while the rest of the mud brick buildings disintegrated and were covered over by the sands and forgotten.

In 1888 the city was discovered by chance when a local villager came across the royal archive, a huge collection of clay tablets. The tablets date mainly to between 1370 and 1350 BC, the short life-span of the city of Amarna. The archive contains the pharaoh's diplomatic correspondence, written in cuneiform, while some was written in a hitherto unknown language, which was subsequently identified as Hittite. The discovery of the clay tablets led Flinders Petrie to begin excavations there in 1891. Further excavations have since taken place, and in 1911-12 a German expedition found a number of statues, plaster casts and portrait heads in the ruins of a sculptor's workshop. However, much lies unexcavated beneath modern fields, mostly in the south, and as the city was lived in for such a short time, it remains a time capsule, uncontaminated by later disturbance.

DISSOLUTION OF THE MONASTERIES, ENGLAND

During the 1530s, Henry VIII effectively abolished the monasteries in England, appropriating most of their wealth for his own use. This Dissolution of the Monasteries has sometimes been viewed as a result of a change in religious attitudes, coinciding as it did with the rise of Protestantism and the establishment of the Church of England. In fact, despite the religious upheaval, the demise of the monasteries at the end of the Medieval period resulted more from the economic realities of the time than from fundamental changes in religion. Throughout the Medieval period in England, monasteries grew steadily in wealth and power. After the Norman Conquest in 1066, William the Conqueror rewarded his followers with grants of land. In their turn, these knights, following the French fashion, began to found religious houses in England, endowing them with some of their newly-won land. It was part of their faith that their souls, and those of their ancestors and descendants, could be saved if a religious community prayed for their salvation in perpetuity, and it was these continuing prayers that the founding of abbeys and priories was designed to procure for their patrons.

The monasteries were able to gain income from several sources, such as by appropriating the receipts of tithes (a type of tax) in their locality. Revenue was also collected from the lands with which the monasteries were endowed, either from farming the land, or

RIGHT *Muchelney Abbey in England was a fairly prosperous monastery. At the beginning of the 16th century the abbot's lodging was rebuilt, but soon after in 1538 the abbey was dissolved, by which time there were only 11 monks. The abbey's estate passed to the Earl of Hertford, and many of the buildings were demolished, while a few were converted to other uses. This well-preserved part of the abbey with its stone tracery is at the south-west corner of the cloister. The doorway once led to the refectory.*

LEFT *Easby Abbey, in England, was founded in 1151 but suffered much damage in the 14th century from English soldiers and Scottish raids. By the end of the 15th century its numbers were declining, and in 1537 it was dissolved. No attempt was made to convert any of the buildings to private use after the Dissolution of the Monasteries. The best preserved building is the frater (refectory) which had an early 13th-century undercroft, and the main frater building above which was rebuilt around 1300.*

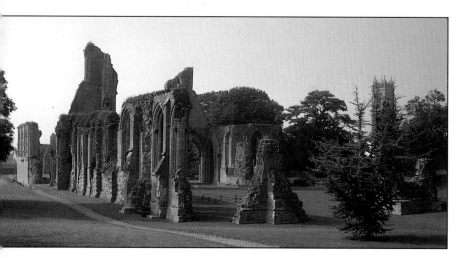

ABOVE *Glastonbury Abbey became the wealthiest monastery in England. It was almost totally destroyed by fire in 1184, but rebuilding began straightaway. The abbey was repeatedly ransacked by Cromwell's commissioners and was finally dissolved in 1539, with the abbot and two monks being executed. For many generations the site was used as a quarry for building stone, in particular for the construction and maintenance of a causeway across the marshes from Glastonbury to Wells.*

from rents from tenant farmers. The shrines of some saints were also a useful source of income since pilgrims visiting these shrines were allowed to buy relaxations of their penances, which were known as indulgences. As they grew in wealth, most monasteries operated on a business basis, owning and operating mills and tanneries for profit, renting out houses, and selling grain, timber, fish, and above all, wool. With the state of their finances largely dependent on the business acumen of the abbots, the fortunes of monasteries fluctuated, and nearly all of them were in debt at some stage in their history, but on balance they prospered, increasing in wealth and becoming major landowners.

The first blow to the prosperity of the monasteries came with the Black Death in 1348. This, with several subsequent plagues, probably halved the population of England. With a greatly reduced labour force on their own and on their tenants' farms, and with a greatly reduced market for the goods and services the monasteries provided, this fall in population was a severe set-back. With labour having become scarce, it also became more expensive, further reducing the profitability of the monasteries, and as their wealth was reduced, so was their power and influence. As early as 1496 the Bishop of Ely obtained permission from the Pope to take possession of the priory of St. Radegunde, near Cambridge. There were only two nuns still living there, and the buildings had become dilapidated. The Bishop founded Jesus College on the site, and the priory church forms the chapel.

A steady trickle of such acquisitions of run-down monasteries gathered strength when Cardinal Wolsey gained Papal permission to dissolve 21 religious houses to finance the foundation of colleges at Oxford and Ipswich. Wolsey was dismissed from his position as Henry VIII's Chancellor in 1530, but his principal aide, Thomas Cromwell, rose to power in the next few years, and it was he who carried through the general Dissolution of the Monasteries. Before the Dissolution, which began with the Act of Suppression in 1536, the monasteries were still considerably wealthy, and between them held nearly a quarter of the land in England. By the time of his death in 1547, Henry VIII had sold most of the monasteries' movable goods and half of their land.

The Dissolution caused the abandonment of most monastery sites, as the purchasers of monastic estates were usually more interested in the land and its produce than in the monastic buildings. Of over 800 monasteries closed at the time of the Dissolution, nearly two-thirds survive as abandoned ruins, although in many instances a small proportion of the buildings on a site were converted to other uses (often farmhouses) or incorporated in later development. In some cases the monastic church has continued in use. Most of the buildings, however, were partly or wholly demolished in order to reuse their building materials, and over a third of the monasteries that were abandoned at the Dissolution have now vanished completely.

BODIE, CALIFORNIA, UNITED STATES OF AMERICA

The effect of market forces are not always so gradual in bringing about the abandonment of sites. In the history of mineral extraction industries, particularly the gold and oil industries, many towns sprang up, flourished for a short period while the industry was booming, and were just as rapidly deserted when the boom was over, leaving abandoned ghost towns, often in desolate and inaccessible places. One such ghost town is Bodie, in California.

From the beginning of the California Gold Rush in 1849 until the opening up of deposits in Alaska and the Klondike fifty years later, thousands of men, many of them immigrants from other countries, came to the region to seek their fortunes. Gold was first found in San Francisco, but later discoveries were made throughout the West, and in their wake many mining towns sprang into existence, in fairly primitive, squalid conditions, and were the home of much gambling and crime. Bodie was one such town, in Mono County, 11km (7 miles) south of Bridgeport, 2400m (8000ft) up in the Sierras and close to the California-Nevada border. The town was named after the discoverer of the ore in 1859, a W S Bodey, and its heyday was from 1876 to 1880, when its population mushroomed to over 10,000, but now it is a totally deserted ghost town. The town was notorious for violence, crime, and gambling, there were 65 saloons, and there was at least one murder a day.

The prime reason for Bodie's existence was gold mining. Early on, the ore-crushing mills, which were supplied by 30 local mines, were driven by steam engines. These engines used wood as fuel, but wood became in short supply and very expensive, and so a hydro-electric plant was built which successfully supplied electricity to the mills. The use of electric power was still in its infancy and the plant was built at Green Creek, 20km (12 miles) from Bodie, since it was thought (but was then untested) that electricity could be supplied over long distances via power lines. The poles were erected in a straight line because of the doubts as to whether electricity could turn corners! There was also a cyanide plant for extracting gold from the ore, which, at the time, was the largest such plant in the United States.

The town had numerous wooden houses, which were flimsily built and which were not well suited to the severe winter weather conditions: temperatures could fall to 40° below zero, winds reach 160kph (100mph) and snow could be 6m (20ft) deep. Consequently much firewood was required for heating, and a small sawmill was established. Not surprisingly in a town of wooden buildings, Bodie suffered fires from time to time. By 1883 Bodie was mostly abandoned as the ores were exhausted, and in 1932 it suffered yet another fire.

Nowadays Bodie is a ghost town, with buildings still lining the streets, and the contents of the streets and buildings left just as they were abandoned. The site was established as a State Historic Park in 1964.

ABOVE Bodie in California, USA, was once a thriving gold mining town, but is now a totally deserted ghost town. In the background is the Standard Mill situated next to the Standard Mine on the west slope of Bodie Bluff. The Mill was destroyed by fire in 1898 but was rebuilt the following year.

LEFT Bodie in California once had a population of over 10,000 people, but is now totally deserted. Instead of being developed for mass tourism, the site is a State Historic Park, preserving the ruins and their contents just as they were abandoned.

ABOVE *The surviving temples at Zawar, India, give an indication of the former wealth of this medieval zinc-smelting site.*

OPPOSITE PAGE *Some of the retorts and perforated clay bricks still in place in a rare example of a 15th-century zinc-smelting furnace at Zawar, India.*

About eighty buildings survive – 1 in 20 of the original buildings at its peak – including the power station, sawmill, a church, schoolhouse, town jail and numerous houses. The vaults of Bodie Bank also survive, but the main building was destroyed by fire in 1932. Instead of being restored, the buildings are being stabilized to prevent further decay, and to prevent modern development designed to cater for tourism, to which all the other ghost towns have been subject. Ironically, the abandoned landscape and fragile ghost town are now being threatened by a major gold mining proposal, as modern methods of cyanide leaching and open-pit mining make this industry economically viable once again.

ZAWAR, INDIA

While some mining settlements, like Bodie, have been abandoned when the ore can no longer be economically extracted, others have suffered a decline because of a dwindling market for the minerals that they produced. This seems to have been the reason for the desertion of Zawar, in India.

Zawar is situated in the Aravalli hills in Rajasthan, about 30 km (19 miles) south of Udaipur. The ancient settlement of Old Zawar lies nearby, beside the Tiri River, surrounded by the dolomite hills from which ores (mainly lead and zinc with some silver and copper) were mined. The site was once a huge industrial settlement for the mining and smelting of zinc, and the surviving remains of this ancient zinc industry are extensive and

unique. Zinc smelting was the main industry, with a small amount of lead smelting. The site certainly seems to have been in production from the 12th to early 19th centuries AD, and possibly a great deal earlier. Mining was undertaken mainly by fire setting: wood fires were lit against the rock face, and then the fires and the rock face were dowsed with water, which caused the rock to shatter. The ore was crushed near the mines before being taken downhill to the valley for smelting. Large amounts of timber survive in the mines, and radiocarbon dates of the wood show that some of these mines are between 2000 and 2500 years old, the earliest known zinc mines in the world.

Not much evidence of the ancient metal production survives in situ, even through the

techniques were very sophisticated. What does survive are enormous heaps of debris. Furnaces usually only lasted for one smelt, and so the frequent replacement of furnaces and refractories led to the accumulation of debris. The main component of these heaps are broken retorts and clay furnace fragments, and the many hundreds of thousands of tonnes of debris suggest an enormous scale of production. Large numbers of spent retorts were also used as hollow bricks in walls, houses and ovens. In the Medieval period in the Punjab, zinc was used for coinage, and there was also a huge demand for zinc for the production of brass. The remains at Zawar suggest that many tens of thousands of tonnes of zinc were produced there.

The heaps of accumulating debris gradually buried old buildings, some to a depth of at least 3m (17ft). Many houses and other buildings survive, some of which were quite impressive. Between the 14th and 16th centuries a large dam, a fort and temples were constructed. There are still five Jain temples on the site, Jainism being largely the religion of the merchant classes. The temples are fairly small but richly adorned, giving a hint of the wealth that the site must have generated when it was flourishing.

By the early 19th century, zinc production is recorded to have ceased completely, with all the mines being flooded. The end probably came in 1812 when a drought caused widespread famine and emigration throughout Rajasthan. However, it is much more likely that this was only the final cause of desertion of the site. Zinc smelting had by this time been developed in China and Europe and the lucrative European markets for zinc had therefore been lost. Zinc was in fact subsequently imported into India for over a century, but just after the Second World War the industry underwent a revival as it became economically viable once more. Thus, for well over five hundred years the fortunes of Zawar have been dictated by changes in the market for zinc.

....
RIGHT *Petra is best known for its rock-cut buildings, mainly temples and tombs, and its distinctive Nabatean architecture. This building, the Khasneh or so-called "treasury" is a temple in Hellenistic style, showing no Nabatean influence, and may have been the work of imported craftsmen.*
....

....
BELOW *A view of the El Deir rock-cut tomb, looking down the Wadi el Deir, one of the many wadis through the sandstone hills.*
....

PETRA, JORDAN

Where a settlement is dependent on a single source of wealth, it is always vulnerable to a change in circumstances. Just as Zawar's fortunes fluctuated with the changes in the zinc market, so Petra's prosperity was based on it being a town on a major trade route. When other routes came to be preferred, with traders no longer passing through the town, Petra went into a decline from which it never recovered.

Petra is one of the most evocative of abandoned places. It lies in southern Jordan, situated in the Wadi Mousa (the Valley of Moses), at the cross-roads of two important trade routes of the ancient world. Petra is bound on two sides by steep sandstone cliffs, themselves cut through by numerous wadis, and one of the advantages of the place was that it had a water supply in the midst of surrounding desert. By the beginning of the 4th century BC the Nabateans had taken control of the area from the Edomites, and Petra became the capital of the Nabatean kingdom. The Nabateans were able to control the trade that passed through Petra, in particular the incense trade from south Arabia to Syria and Palestine, and the city became a thriving commercial centre.

Petra is most well-known for its architectural remains, including numerous rock-cut tombs and inscriptions, and architectural study and epigraphy have been complemented by archaeological excavation. The early Nabatean architecture was fairly simple, but it gradually developed, and from

the 2nd century BC it began to be influenced by Hellenistic ideas. Numerous temples were constructed as well as tombs, cut into the soft sandstone, their facades carved with Hellenistic architectural features. The Nabateans also carried out complex water engineering, constructing cisterns and conduits and installing earthenware pipes to ensure a reliable water supply. The later architecture was influenced by Roman ideas, and in AD 106 the Nabatean territory, including Petra, became a Roman province. From the 2nd or 3rd century AD trade began to pass through Palmyra, a city to the north, and the traders gradually abandoned Petra, which led to its decline. However, the city may have survived for many more decades, and may even have been inhabited until the 6th century. It is suggested that the final destruction of Petra occurred in the catastrophic earthquake which wrecked both Jerusalem and Jerash in the mid 8th century AD.

The Crusaders built a small fort on the summit of one of the rock outcrops known as el Habis, the remains of which can be seen, but after that the city remained utterly abandoned, surviving only as a legend. The desert tribes gradually took over the city, using the tombs as caves for habitation – right up to 1986. Petra was rediscovered in 1812 by Jean Louis Burckhardt, who was travelling through the region disguised as an Arab for safety. The local Arab tribes believed that treasure was hidden throughout Petra, and so were extremely suspicious of any visitors. Several years later Petra was immortalized by John William Burgon, with the words:

"Match me such marvel in Eastern clime,
A rose-red city – 'half as old as time'".

At that time, the world was thought to be 6000 years old, and Petra was thought to be half its age – that is, 'half as old as time'. Today, there are extensive remains for the visitor to see, but these are largely the tombs on the edge of the city – of the city itself, situated on the wide valley floor, very few visible remains survive.

GREAT ZIMBABWE, ZIMBABWE

In the case of Petra, it is easy to understand what led to its decline and abandonment, but with other sites the situation is more complex and it is difficult to isolate a dominant factor that has caused the decline of the settlement. At the site of Great Zimbabwe, for instance, it is not clear whether over-exploitation of resources or a shift in the trading pattern finally led to its abandonment, yet both factors undoubtedly played a part in its decline.

In 1871, Carl Mauch, a German explorer, discovered the overgrown ruins of Great Zimbabwe, then being partly used as a cattle kraal. There are gold deposits in the vicinity, and the site once exported gold. Stories of gold in the region had passed into legend. Mauch and subsequent explorers believed that the ruins were associated with the biblical Queen of Sheba and King Solomon, and was possibly the site of King Solomon's mines. A romantic version of their discovery was the basis of Rider Haggard's novel *King Solomon's Mines*. The ruins were certainly not

considered to have been constructed by the native population, since stone was regarded as a hallmark of "civilized" societies. Later work by archaeologists showed that the ruins had in fact been built by local tribes, probably between the 10th and 15th centuries AD. This caused much political controversy with the ruling white population, who did not believe that the native population could have been responsible for such sophisticated architecture.

Great Zimbabwe is situated on a high granite plateau, within the country of the Shona-speaking people. From their language came the word *zimbabwe*, meaning either a venerated house, the dwelling of a chief, or houses of stone, and Great Zimbabwe was the largest of over 200 zimbabwe on the plateau. The first settlement from the 4th-5th century AD was on a fairly small scale, but in about AD 1200 the Early Iron Age agricultural village began to be replaced by a larger settlement with stone walls, and had begun to be a trading settlement.

Great Zimbabwe consists of numerous walls built without mortar from the abundant local granite, with the later walls being much more sophisticated in their construction. The settlement was at its peak in the 14th and 15th centuries AD as trade increased and most new building took place, and Great Zimbabwe came to cover 40 hectares (100 acres). There were three main areas – the Hill Ruin (once called the Acropolis), the Valley Ruins and the Elliptical Building or Great Enclosure. None of these were in fact buildings, but unroofed stone-walled enclosures adjoining which were numerous clay-walled, thatched huts (daga huts) which have left no surface trace. The Elliptical Building gradually evolved from a small enclosure to one with a massive encircling wall up to 10m (33ft) high and 5m (16ft) thick. Within the Elliptical Building is a conical tower, 9m (30ft) high and 5.5m (18ft) diameter, the purpose of which is unknown. This enclosure housed the settlement of the king and his relatives.

At the height of its prosperity, Great Zimbabwe may have had a population of some 10,000 people (the figures are disputed). It began its life as a farming community, but by the 14th century it was a thriving and powerful city, trading in gold and other raw materials with its African neighbours and the east African coastal settlements. Gold, copper and iron were worked at the settlement, and soapstone was carved to make dishes and sculptures. Many fine objects have been found at the site, showing that in return for exports, imported goods from as far afield as China reached Great Zimbabwe. The weaving of textiles must also have taken place as numerous spindle whorls have been discovered.

In about AD 1450 power shifted to the north, and in particular Kilwa assumed importance as a trading centre. It is suggested that this shift of power may be because Great Zimbabwe had declined due to agricultural over-exploitation of the area, having supported so many inhabitants. Certainly from the middle of the 15th century Great

....
PREVIOUS PAGE *A view of Great Zimbabwe showing the Elliptical Building, a massive enclosure with drystone walls 10m high, inside which was a conical tower.*
....

Zimbabwe declined and it was probably abandoned by the late 16th century, although it probably continued as a venerated site. Today it is a national monument.

EASTER ISLAND, SOUTH PACIFIC

The factors which led to the decline of an astonishing culture at Easter Island may also have been man-made, namely, the exhaustion of the island's natural resources – but Easter Island itself remains an enigma.

Easter Island (Isla de Pascua) is 2500km (1550 miles) from the Pacific coast of Chile and 2000km (1200 miles) from the closest inhabited islands of Polynesia. It is a small, hilly, treeless island of volcanic origin, with an area of only 115sq.km (44 sq. miles), so

ABOVE Over 400 stone statues have been found on Easter Island. They each weigh up to 100 tonnes. In the late 18th century and early 19th century many statues were pushed over face downwards, while others were left unfinished. The population declined and the island was virtually depopulated after 1862.

remote that it was not discovered by Europeans until Easter Day, 1722. The island was first settled by Polynesians in about AD 400, and may once have had a population of up to 7000 people. The earliest settlers built huge stone platforms and carved life-size stone figures. Between AD 700 and 1700 numerous giant stone statues were carved from single blocks of stone, which must have required a great deal of labour for quarrying and carving, and the use of many lengths of timber for transporting the statues, which weighed up to 100 tonnes. The statues were carved in situ at the quarry, and their backs were then detached from the quarry face. They were transported down the quarry and set up in pits to enable the backs to be carved and polished, and were then taken to and erected on carved ceremonial stone

platforms, known as *ahus*. Apart from over 400 stone statues, numerous *petroglyphs* (rock carvings) are also found all over the island, but their connection with the statues is not clear. All the carving was done with stone tools. A number of wooden tablets with inscriptions have also been found on the island, although the script has yet to be deciphered.

The strain on the island's resources, and in particular the deforestation of the island, may well have been the main cause of the ultimate decline of the culture, whose people were no longer able to produce sufficient food and timber. The island and its culture remain an enigma in the world's prehistory, but it appears that in the late 18th and early 19th centuries all the statues were pushed over face downwards, and many still

ABOVE *Easter Island is a small remote volcanic island in the Pacific. Here large statues were carved between AD 700 and 1700 and were set up on 'ahus' – carved ceremonial stone platforms.*

stood unfinished and partly buried inside and outside the crater rim of Rano Raraku, where they were being carved. The population declined, and virtually died out in 1862 after a Peruvian slave raid which was followed by a smallpox epidemic.

CHANG'AN, CHINA

More complex even than the factors determining the fate of Great Zimbabwe and Easter Island are the events which have influenced the history of the Chinese settlement of Chang'an. From 206 BC Chang'an (the City of Enduring Peace) was the capital of the Western Han dynasty, and the ruins of the Han city wall can be seen about 7km (4 miles) to the north-west of X'ian city centre. The city measured approximately 6.5km x 6.5km (4 × 4 miles), and was protected by an encircling wall with 12 gates. It was a prosperous city and a cultural centre, but in the early 1st century AD it was attacked and taken, and subsequently lost its position as capital in favour of Lo-yang to the east. From the late 2nd century Chang'an suffered attacks, pillaging and massacres as China was plunged into chaos and unrest.

In AD 589 China was reunited with the foundation of the Sui dynasty, and a new capital was established to the south of the Han city of Chang'an. In AD 607–10 this political unity was strengthened by the construction of a series of canals linking three cities, including Chang'an, with the Yellow River. In AD 618 the Sui dynasty gave way to the T'ang dynasty which marked a beginning of expansion of the empire, and a period of prosperity and peace. The T'ang capital continued to be at Chang'an, and much of the building and layout of the city dates from this period. It became the cultural and economic centre of its vast empire, and in the 7th and 8th centuries the city was a huge cosmopolitan metropolis, the world's most populous city with over one million people. The main city walls enclosed an area of 84sq.km (32sq. miles)

Chang'an was the eastern terminus of the Silk Route, and was a great trading city, with over 100 merchant guilds – its markets sold all types of everyday and exotic goods. Silver coins from Byzantium and Persia have been found during excavations, and the ruts left by waggons 1200 years ago also bear witness to busy traffic and trade. The city was built on a grid plan and was divided into a hundred or more residential wards. The two chief markets and the residential wards were each surrounded by a wall with gates, locked at night to maintain absolute control of the citizens. The layout of Chang'an became a model for cities as far afield as Japan.

Most of the buildings were of tamped earth and timber construction, and like many of China's ancient cities, virtually nothing survives above ground. Two pagodas of this period do survive: the Great Goose Pagoda was built in 652, and the Small Goose Pagoda, made of brick, was constructed in 707, and these pagodas are referred to in literature of the T'ang period. The absence of physical visible remains is in contrast to cities of the

Middle East where monumental architecture and sculpture often survives. Paradoxically, though, as well as literary references, a complete plan of the city is shown on ancient maps, and consequently much of the layout and identification of the buildings of the city is known. Intensive excavations have also added to this picture. To the north of Chang'an are impressive colossal royal tombs, yet to be excavated.

By the early 8th century, Chang'an was heavily dependent on huge shipments of grain from other regions. During the 8th century there was a considerable population loss from north to south China following warfare, climatic disaster and plague. The T'ang dynasty was destroyed by internal rebellions from 874 onwards. In the 880s Chang'an was practically razed, and with continuing rebellions and civil strife in the late 9th century, this north-west region of China declined into an economic and political backwater. Chang'an declined with it and was largely abandoned.

Nowadays part of the site is the modern city of X'ian, capital of the Shaanxi province, and dates mainly from the Ming period (15th–17th century), when the city was built on the original palace site. The city is still surrounded by its original walls, although much repaired. For more than 8km (5 miles) to the south stretches farmland which once formed part of Chang'an. The farm roads still follow the line of the ancient roads, and occasional mounds and dressed stones give hints of the once huge and thriving metropolis.

Changing Landscapes

LEFT *The Horyuji temple complex in the Nara Basin is the oldest completely preserved temple complex in Japan, and although located some distance north of Asuka, is a fine example of the architecture of the Asuka period (AD 552–645). The five-storey pagoda is 32 m (105 ft) high and stands in a courtyard. On the left is the Kondo (Main Hall), the oldest wooden building in the world, founded in AD 607 along with the temple.*

RIGHT *The appearance of an abandoned place today may be no indication of its past appearance, particularly where civilisations used mud-brick construction which can disintegrate rapidly. This flat, featureless landscape is the site of a large new city built along the River Nile by King Akhenaten in about 1370 BC.*

Landscapes are not static. The combination of natural forces and the effects of human activity create a landscape that is continually changing. Early hunting and gathering communities constantly moved from site to site in search of a food supply, but the evidence for their temporary settlements is at best ephemeral. Any effect that these hunter-gatherers had on the landscape soon disappeared because the population was small and their activities made little impression. As populations grew larger, though, their impact on the environment became increasingly more noticeable. With the development of farming, communities became more settled, forced by a continuous cycle of growing seasons to remain in one spot, at least until the fertility of the soil was exhausted and the place had to be abandoned. As people became more proficient farmers, societies grew up and gradually became more complex. Civilizations developed, and settlements were established for reasons other than agriculture – for trade, industry, defence, or for political and religious motives. Settlements were quite often deliberately founded or expanded by a controlling ruling class, more often for the aggrandizement of the rulers than for more practical reasons.

Whatever the purpose of the settlement, each town and city, each industrial or farming site, and each house or hovel leaves a mark on the landscape. Such scars take time to heal – often many centuries – and there are relatively few places left on the planet where mankind has not made a mark at some stage in history. The changing landscapes that we see now are composed of today's inhabited areas and yesterday's abandoned places – today's societies are often, quite literally, built on the ruins of yesterday's civilizations.

An abandoned site may present a picture of a mass of stone ruins with fine architectural remains, or else a forlorn expanse of featureless landscape with no visible sign of a previous civilization. What a site looks like today is no guide to its former fortunes and appearance. Chang'an in China, for example, had virtually no stone buildings, and so virtually nothing survives above ground. Yet in the 7th and 8th centuries AD, it was a thriving cosmopolitan city with many poets, writers, musicians and artists, and was a centre of Buddhism. Information about what a site was like is derived from the careful

ABOVE *The Maya site at Uxmal in Mexico still displays evidence of its impressive architecture. The main structures include the Monjas or Nunnery, four long buildings round a huge quadrangle, and behind it the Pyramid of the Magician. The city began to flourish from the 7th century, but was abandoned around the year 1000.*

processes of survey and the study of surviving architecture, inscriptions and documents. An excavation of a site can also yield a considerable amount of additional information, including evidence for the environment.

The study and excavation of a site may also show why and when the site was abandoned, particularly where the visible signs are fairly obvious – such as the forceful destruction at San Lorenzo in Mexico or the devastating fire at Cowdray House in England. More often, though, the history of a site is extremely complex, and instead of coming to a final and sudden end, civilizations tend to wax and wane over long periods of time. The rise and fall of civilizations, and with it the abandonment of their settlements, is a constant recurring theme throughout prehistory and history. Today it just seems astonishing that so many powerful civilizations could end, some leaving behind virtually no visible trace.

SETTLEMENT CHANGE IN JAPAN

It is not usually possible to examine one particular site and explain why it was abandoned without looking at it in its context – both in terms of its surrounding landscape and the politics of the day. One example of the constant abandonment of sites is in Japan. There the power of the rulers was such that they could quite literally have vast new capitals and palaces constructed at will, so that whole populations had to move. Asuka is the site of a city which lies in the south-west part of the Nara Basin (otherwise known as the Yamato Plain) 25km (15 miles) south of the present-day city of Nara. In AD 592 the Empress Suiko built the Toyura palace there, and Asuka remained the political and religious capital of the country throughout the 7th century. There were numerous temples and imperial tombs, and the first full-scale Buddhist temple to be built in Japan was the Asukadera.

The Empress Jitō (AD 646-703) was the 41st ruler and succeeded the Emperor Temmu in AD 686 until the Emperor Mommu was old enough to take the throne in 697. The Empress took the major step of setting up a new capital city at Fujiwarakyo, with an adjoining palace to the north surrounded by a colonnaded cloister. After several years of construction, she set up residence there in 694. The new city was Japan's first grid plan city, modelled along the lines of the Chinese capital of Chang'an, with rectangular blocks of buildings separated by straight roads. The country roads nowadays still follow the original grid lines. Excavations have taken place since 1934, the finds including some 2,000 inscribed wooden tallies (called *mokkan*).

At Asuka only caretakers remained to look after the dilapidated temples, but by the 9th century the site had been abandoned and ricefields encroached on the remains. Just below the surface were traces of successive palaces, temples and houses, and even a few unlooted tombs on the hillside. Only since the 1950s have archaeological excavations been taking place, revealing the outlines of many temples and palaces.'The Asukadera continued in use for a time, but in 1196 it was partly destroyed by fire, which led to its ultimate deterioration.

The Emperor Mommu died after only a short reign in AD 707. As the emperor-to-be Shōmu was only 7 years old, Mommu's wife the Empress Gemmyō (662-722) was put on the throne. She is best known for transferring the capital 18km (11 miles) northwards from Fujiwarakyo, after it had been in use as a city for only 16 years. Two years were spent marking out the new city of Heijokyo and

constructing the palaces. The whole city was moved from Fujiwarakyo to Heijokyo in AD 710, along with the 30,000 or more inhabitants. The major temples of Fujiwarakyo were dismantled and re-erected at Heijokyo. The site at Fujiwarakyo is said in later writings to have been destroyed by fire in AD 711.

The area in which Heijokyo was built had been inhabited for a long period, and so numerous tombs had to be levelled. The city covered an area of about 4.8km x 4.3km (3 × 2.7 miles), and by the end of the 8th century the population is thought to have risen to about 200,000. It was laid out on a square grid pattern, with two palaces in the north for alternative use, a pair of markets in the south, and seven major and nine minor temples.

In the 8th century there were two occasions on which the capital was nearly moved again, but was saved by portentous

....
ABOVE *The Great Buddha Hall at the Todaiji temple still houses a huge bronze statue of the Great Buddha.*
....
RIGHT *The Todaiji was an immense temple complex built by the Emperor Shomu on the eastern edge of the city of Heijokyo, in Japan. It included the Great Buddha Hall, the largest wooden building ever to be constructed in the world. This building was burned in the civil war in 1180, rebuilt, burned again in 1567, and again rebuilt.*
....

warnings. Subsequently, the Emperor Shōmu had an immense temple complex built, the Todaiji, on the eastern edge of the city. It was begun in 745 and dedicated in 752, and included the Great Buddha Hall, the largest wooden building ever to be constructed in the world, which still houses a huge bronze statue of the Great Buddha. This building was burned in the civil war in 1180, rebuilt by the priest Chōgen, burned again in 1567, and was again rebuilt. The Todaiji temple served as the headquarters of a network of Buddhist monasteries and nunneries. The Shosoin, the Imperial Treasure House, was also located at the temple, and is still standing today, complete with its rare 8th century treasures.

In 784 the Emperor Kammu moved the capital yet again, this time further north to Nagaoko, and so yet again another city was abandoned. By 864 it is reported that the buildings and roads of Heijokyo had disappeared and reverted to fields. The survival of the temples, though, ensured that the site remained a place of pilgrimage. The modern city of Nara grew up on the hillside on the east of Heijokyo, and much of the old city, often referred to as Nara, reverted to flat open ricefields and villages. Archaeologists have excavated at Heijokyo for many years, and have fully exposed the easternmost of the two palaces, which is now preserved as a park. Many objects of daily use have been discovered, including numerous wooden artefacts and some 20,000 inscribed wooden tax tallies (*mokkan*) dated to between 709 and 782. They were tied onto goods during transport, and so have created a

record showing the arrival of many goods at the palace, giving an insight into the tax system.

TROY, TURKEY

The constant moving of settlements in Japan was for political and religious reasons, yet without the evidence from contemporary and later accounts, it would be much more difficult for archaeologists to unravel the complex history of that region. It is only with the advent of writing that the evidence from archaeological survey and excavations can be integrated with the evidence derived from written sources. In the 19th century Schliemann was determined to find the site of Homer's Troy, which many people believed to be a fictional place. He finally decided to excavate at the mound of Hissarlik in Turkey which is now accepted by most people as the site of Troy. In fact, the site of Hissarlik is very complex, and the methods of excavation used by Schliemann were not best suited to unravelling its history. Over 46 levels of occupation and 9 cities or settlements have been identified, spanning a period from about 3000 BC to AD 400 – not just one Troy but several.

In it heyday, the place was very wealthy, profiting from trade, particularly as it then overlooked the sea. The first settlement, Troy I, was less than 90m (100yd) in diameter, but it had a substantial enclosure wall of mud brick on stone foundations. It was founded in about 3000 BC on a promontory overlooking the sea, but was destroyed by fire in 2500 BC.

A much wealthier fortified citadel, Troy II, was then constructed, with substantial buildings. The so-called Priam's treasure was found at this level, and Schliemann thought that this was Homer's Troy, but in fact the dates for it are far too early. Troy II was destroyed by fire in about 2200 BC, probably in an attack. Troy III to V lasted from about 2300 BC to 1800 BC, and was a relatively small, less wealthy settlement, with smaller houses. Troy VI was established around 1800 BC by newcomers who constructed a fortification wall enclosing an area of 2 hectares (5 acres). The city was wealthy and there is evidence of much trade. In about 1275 BC it was destroyed in an earthquake. Troy VIIa (1275 BC to 1240 BC) was a poorer settlement; the walls appear to have been rapidly rebuilt after the earthquake, but the site was destroyed soon after. This may have been the time of Homer's Trojan War. The site was re-occupied, but it was again destroyed and finally abandoned in 1100 BC.

Troy was not re-occupied until about 700 BC when Greek colonists from the island of Lesbos established a settlement there. In the time of Alexander the Great, several new buildings were erected, but about 82 BC the colony was destroyed in the Mithridatic wars. It was rebuilt by the Romans in the mid 1st century BC and was called Ilium Novum. The walls and a theatre can still be seen. Troy was an episcopal see in the 4th century AD, but it then declined, probably because of the silting up of the harbour. Up to 1500 there was very small-scale occupation of the site, but this was followed by total abandonment.

ABOVE *In the mid 1st century BC the Greek colony at Troy was destroyed in the Mithridatic wars, but it was rebuilt by the Romans in the mid 1st century BC.*

LEFT *The level of occupation known as Troy VI was established around 1800 BC. This settlement was quite wealthy and there was much trade, but in about 1275 BC it was destroyed in an earthquake, to be replaced by a much poorer settlement.*

chapter seven

Abandonment Today

Complex patterns of destruction, rebuilding and abandonment, such as at Troy, still take place today. Current political and economic pressures can still cause the abandonment of places for a whole variety of reasons, particularly in countries with strictly observed ideologies. In Romania, for example, there has been a programme of demolishing thousands of historic villages in order to rehouse the people in large agro-industrial centres, in order to eliminate differences between urban and rural society. On a lesser scale, buildings and landscapes are abandoned and destroyed almost daily in order to construct reservoirs, dams and new roads.

Natural disasters are just as likely to cause the abandonment of sites today as in the past, particularly if it is impossible for rebuilding to take place. The eruption of the volcano at Mt St Helens in the United States was predicted, and so small communities in the area were able to leave well in advance. The eruption was of such a magnitude, though, that areas previously inhabited were totally buried. Similarly, the nuclear disaster at Chernobyl in the USSR, although man-made,

caused an environmental catastrophe that has forced the abandonment of much productive agricultural land and settlements in the surrounding region. In time, this region may once again become populated, and the present interlude may not even show as an identifiable period of abandonment in the archaeological record.

Increasingly, the damage to the environment in many parts of the world threatens to bring about the abandonment of whole regions. Over-exploitation of agricultural land can cause a dust-bowl effect, while the devastation of forests and the pollution of the air is changing the climate, causing severe drought and dessication in some areas. In the USSR, the Aral Sea used to be Asia's second largest lake, 65,000sq.km (25,000sq. miles) in area. The diversion of water from two main rivers as part of a policy of irrigation of farmland for increased production has led to the Aral Sea shrinking in size – so far to about half its original area. This is causing an environmental disaster in the region. Fishing communities are now a long way from the lake, increased salinity is poisoning the wildlife and the agricultural

LEFT *In many countries places can still become abandoned for political and economic reasons. This ghost town near the ancient mound of Jericho was abandoned by the Palestinians when the Israelis occupied the West Bank.*

land, the climate is changing, and places like Aralsk are becoming depopulated.

With the changing climate and the so-called "greenhouse effect", it could be that, instead of abandonment of sites on a fairly small-scale as has happened in the past, huge areas could become arid desert, while low-lying areas such as Pacific islands may become totally submerged, leading not just to the abandonment of individual places, but of whole regions. In the early stages, mankind had no influence on the environment, and left little imprint on the landscape. Now there are many powerful forces affecting the environment, and if these are not controlled wisely, the human population is likely to suffer much more than it did when the environment was totally beyond its control.

....
LEFT Natural disasters are just as likely to cause abandonment of sites today as in the past. The eruption of Mt St Helens in USA was predicted, so small communities in the area were able to be evacuated well in advance.
....

Glossary

agora: large open area with a surrounding complex of buildings in an ancient Greek town which functioned as a market place, meeting place, and the social, commercial, political and legal centre of the town.

ahus: carved ceremonial rectangular stone platforms found on Easter Island as the base for large stone statues.

Aten: the sun's disc, worshipped as a deity by the ancient Egyptians. Unlike other Egyptian cults, the Aten cult was a short-lived monotheistic cult, where the god was not portrayed in anthropomorphic form, but only as a sun disc with radiating rays.

Black Douglas: one of two branches of the clan of the Earls of Douglas, the other being the Red Douglas.

bouleuterion: hall or council chamber of an ancient Greek city in which the meetings of the council took place.

Bronze Age: period of prehistory when bronze was used as the main material for making tools. Since this occurred at different times in different places, dating of the Bronze Age varies: in Europe it generally dates to the early 1st millenium bc, while in Western Asia it dates to the 3rd and 2nd millenia BC.

Covenanters: signatories to the National Covenant drawn up in Scotland in 1638. This was an anti-Catholic movement for religious and political reforms, which led to civil war in Scotland.

cuneiform: an early writing system of impressions made on clay tablets with a wedge-shaped stylus. Originally used for writing in the Sumerian language, it was subsequently adapted for other languages such as Hittite and Old Persian.

dendrochronology: a method of dating wood by counting annual growth rings (tree rings).

Druids: a Celtic priesthood, powerful at the time of the Roman conquest of Britain and Gaul.

gsur: (singular, *gasr*) arabic name for stone "castles" or fortified farms, found in the Sahara desert.

iwan: an open-fronted vaulted room or hall facing onto a courtyard in a Persian palace.

kiva: an underground room, generally circular in plan, used for ritual purposes in Pueblo settlements.

Maya: a Mesoamerican culture centred on Mexico and Guatemala, dating from before AD 300 to at least AD 900.

mokkan: ancient Japanese tax-tallies inscribed on strips of wood.

petroglyphs: carvings on rock, quite often prehistoric in date.

photogrammetry: the science of measuring from photographs, used particularly in making maps and recording buildings.

Pliny the Younger: (*c.* AD 61–112) nephew and adopted son of Pliny the Elder, who died at Pompeii. He is best known for his published books of letters, which give first-hand information about his life and times.

prytaneion: official headquarters of the committee which formed the administration of an ancient Greek city.

pueblos: adjoining rectangular rooms, often built in several storeys, found particularly in south-west United States.

stela: an upright stone slab or column, often decorated with carvings or inscriptions.

stupa: a tomb of a Buddhist holy man found throughout southern Asia. Usually a domed structure of stone or brick with a surrounding decorated railing, often the focus of a monastery.

Tacitus: (*c.* AD 55–120) distinguished orator, politician and historian of imperial Rome; best known for his historical writing.

tell: a mound formed from the accumulation of debris resulting from the continuous settlement of a site, usually in areas where mud-brick was the main building material.

Terp (pl. Terpen): artificial mounds on which settlements were built in the low-lying areas of Holland and Germany to avoid flooding. The mounds gradually increased in size due to accumulated animal and domestic debris. Also called Wurten or Wierden.

Wurten or Wierden: see terp.

Xenophon: (*c.* 428–354 BC) in his youth a follower of Socrates. He was a prolific writer on many subjects, but is best remembered as a Greek historian.

ziggurat: large stepped temple towers of the Mesopotamian civilizations, probably symbolizing mountains, the residence of the gods.

zimbabwe: stone-built enclosures found in southern Africa, the most well-known being Great Zimbabwe.

Further Reading

L & R Adkins 1989 *An Introduction to Archaeology* (The Apple Press, London and Chartwell Books, Secaucus, New Jersey) Introduction to the techniques that archaeologists use to discover, explore and interpret abandoned places.

J Audric 1972 *Angkor and the Khmer Empire* (Robert Hale, London). Detailed account of the history of Angkor and its remains.

I Browning 1973 *Petra* (Chatto & Windus). Detailed, readable account of Petra – its history and its architecture.

MD Coe 1984 *Mexico* (Thames & Hudson). Readable illustrated book on early civilizations in Mexico.

PS Garlake 1973 *Great Zimbabwe* (Thames & Hudson). A description of the ruins at Great Zimbabwe, early work on the site and the political controversy.

E Kidder 1977 *Ancient Japan* (Elsevier-Phaidon). Useful illustrated account of Japan's early prehistory and history.

SA Matheson 1976 *Persia: an Archaeological Guide* (Faber, 2nd ed). Detailed description of many of the estimated 250,000 surviving ancient sites in modern-day Iran.

P Matthiae 1977 *Ebla. An Empire Rediscovered* (Hodder & Stoughton). Gives an account of excavations at Tell Mardikh, and the important discoveries.

B Norman 1987 *Footsteps. Nine Archaeological Journeys of Romance and Discovery* (BBC Books). Fascinating account of early discoveries of some major sites across the world.

P Rawson 1977 *Indian Asia* (Elsevier-Phaidon). Well-illustrated introduction to many of the early monuments in places like India, Thailand and Cambodia.

C Scarre (ed) 1988 *Past Worlds: the Times Atlas of Archaeology* (Times Books). Well illustrated descriptions of many ancient civilizations, with numerous maps.

Acknowledgements

Several people have helped in the writing of this book and in the search for suitable pictures. Sources of pictures are listed under picture credits. We would also like to thank California Department of Parks and Recreation; Paul Craddock (The British Museum); I. Noël Hume (the Colonial Williamsburg Foundation); Donna Pozzi (Save Bodie!) campaign; John Schofield (Museum of London); and Frank Stanford.

The authors and publishers would like to thank Penguin Books Ltd for permission to reproduce 14 lines from 'The Ruin' in *The Earliest English Poems* translated by Michael Alexander (Penguin Classics, Second Edition, 1977), © Michael Alexander, 1966, 1967, on page 7 and The Literary Estate of the late Sir Charles Johnston to reproduce his poem on page 24.

Picture Credits

Lesley and Roy Adkins: pages 8, 10, 12, 20, 22, 23, 50, 51, 84, 85, 86, 87, 88, 96 and 97.
M E Baines/J Bell: pages 21 and 24.
Julian Bowsher: pages 9, 19 and 92.
Courtesy of the Trustees of the British Museum: pages 100 and 101.
California Department of Parks and Recreation: pages 13 and 99.
The Chilean Consulate General: pages 107 and 108.
DAS Photo: pages 53, 102, 103 and 118.
Douglas Dickeins Photo Library: pages 15, 17, 46, 56, 57, 59, 60, 62, 110 and 115.
C M Dixon: pages 6, 11 left, 27, 29 bottom, 42, 43, 44, 71, 72, 77, 78, 80 and 94 bottom.
Geoscience Features Picture Library: pages 11 right, 16, 45, 83 and 105.
Alan Gilbert: pages 64, 65, 116 and 117.
Peter Hinton: page 82.

Japan National Tourist Organization: page 114.
Scott McCracken: pages 94 and 111.
Simon McCudden: page 55.
The High Commission for Pakistan: pages 28 and 29 top.
Pilkington Glass Museum: page 95.
Polorbis Travel Ltd: page 38.
John Schofield: pages 89, 90 and 91.
Mick Sharp: © Richard Bryant: pages 35, 36, 48, 49 and 112.
    © Jim Killgore: pages 26, 30 and 32.
    © Dave Longley: pages 25, 74, 76, 79 and 81.
    © Mick Sharp: pages 67, 68, 69, 70 and 73.
    © Roger Simpson: pages 40 and 41.
Simon Stoddart/Caroline Malone: pages 18 and 31.
United States Travel & Tourism Administration: pages 14 and 120/121.

Index

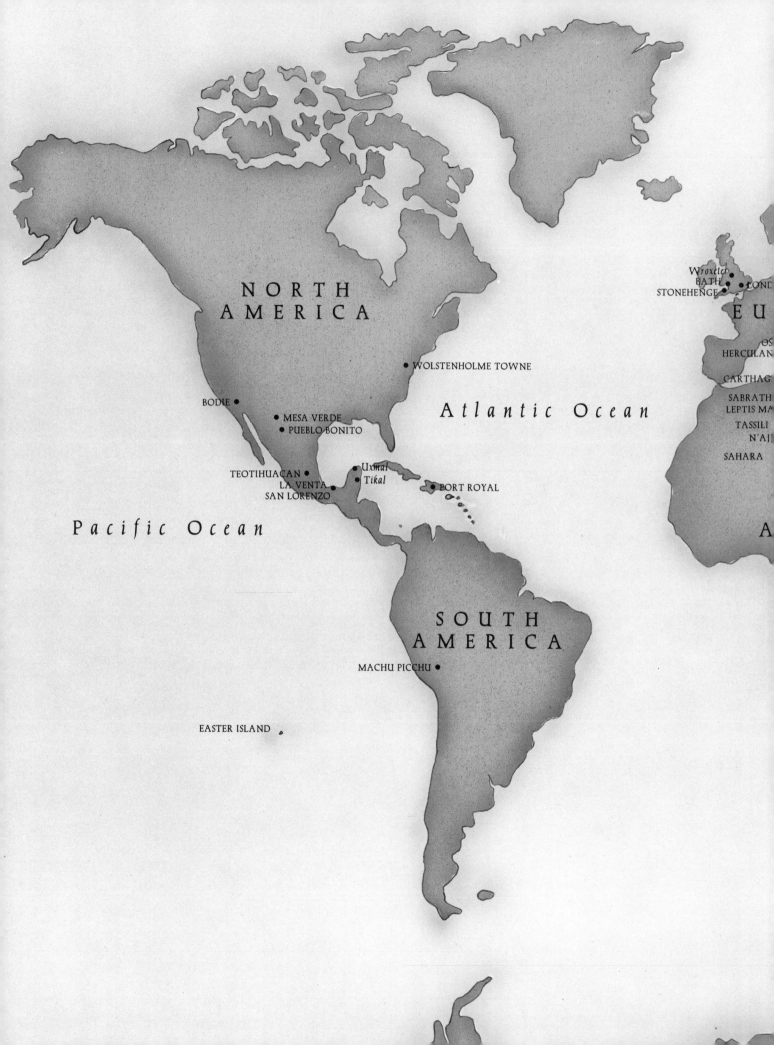

NORTH
AMERICA

Atlantic Ocean

WOLSTENHOLME TOWNE

BODIE

MESA VERDE
PUEBLO BONITO

TEOTIHUACAN
Uxmal
Tikal
LA VENTA
SAN LORENZO

PORT ROYAL

Pacific Ocean

SOUTH
AMERICA

MACHU PICCHU

EASTER ISLAND

Wroxeter
BATH
STONEHENGE LOND

EU

OS
HERCULAN

CARTHAG

SABRATH
LEPTIS MA

TASSILI
N'AJ

SAHARA

A